W9-CPB-593

The Teachings of Pope John Paul II

Summaries of Papal Documents

*To Fr. Ed
Best wishes,
John E. Fagan
3/28/06*

John E. Fagan

 Scepter

Copyright 2005. John E. Fagan

Scepter Publishers
PO Box 211
New York NY 10018

ISBN: 1-59417-045-2

Contents.

Encyclicals.

Apostolic Exhortations.

Apostolic Letters.

Letters.

Bull of Indiction.

Pontifical Council on the Family.

Contents   v

Preface

The teachings of Pope John Paul II will be a source of permanent enrichment for the Church and the world. During his long pontificate, he issued an extraordinary number of documents on every aspect of Christianity. It will take theologians decades to digest this legacy. Just reading all of the Holy Father's encyclicals, apostolic exhortations and other major documents is an ambitious undertaking. Unfortunately, the demands on the time of many lay people are such that doing so is not a realistic possibility.

The purpose of this volume is to make the Pope's teachings more accessible to busy lay people. The summaries that follow are intended to serve only as introductions to the respective papal documents. Needless to say, such short summaries cannot do justice to John Paul's writings. I have tried to emphasize the aspects that I believe are of greatest interest to lay people. I have relied heavily on the Holy Father's own words and have attempted to keep my own commentary to a minimum. I hope that, after reading one of the summaries, the reader will then read and reflect on the entire document. If that is not possible, however, at least the reader will have had some exposure to the Pope's message.

These summaries originated as outlines for monthly talks given to groups of laymen before and after the workday. My objective was to cover as much material as possible within the limited time available.

I hope the summaries will be useful, not only for the readers' personal reflection, but also as an aid to those who desire to organize talks or discussion groups to further disseminate the Holy Father's teachings.

The complete texts of the Holy Father's documents may be found on the Vatican web site at www.vatican.va.

I am sure the readers will join me in giving thanks to God for the great doctrinal treasure that has been bequeathed to the Church by Pope John Paul II.

J.E.F.
Reston, Virginia
December 8, 2005

Redemptor Hominis
(The Redeemer of Man.)
Encyclical Letter dated March 4, 1979.

In *Redemptor Hominis,* his first encyclical, Pope John Paul II provides an outline of the program for his pontificate. He makes it clear in the first paragraph that he believes his special mission is to prepare the Church to enter the Third Christian Millennium. He calls the years remaining before the year 2000 a "new Advent," a time of extended preparation for the Jubilee. He urges the faithful to direct themselves — mind, heart and will — towards Christ the Redeemer during this period (n. 7).*

This encyclical includes sections on many of the topics that will be the subjects of separate encyclicals or apostolic exhortations later in John Paul's pontificate such as Christian unity, the Church's apostolic mission, reconciliation and penance, faith and reason, and the role of the laity. The primary focus of *Redemptor Hominis,* however, is the mystery of man as revealed in Jesus Christ.

The Mystery of the Redemption.

The Pope begins the encyclical with the words, "The Redeemer of man, Jesus Christ, is the center of the universe and of history" (n. 1). By redeeming us, Christ liberated us from the slavery of sin and made it possible for us to live as children of God. As such, we can participate in the interior life of God through grace.

Beginning his pontificate in the final quarter of the twentieth century, the Holy Father reflects on

* The numbers in parentheses refer to the paragraph numbers of the document.

the lessons mankind learned during the century. He maintains that in the twentieth century the "futility" to which the world has been subjected since the original sin (cf., Rom. 8: 20) was once again clearly demonstrated. Many people believed that a maturing humanity had outgrown its need for religion and that the world could be organized without God. Those who tried to do so, however, brought repeated catastrophe upon mankind in one of the bloodiest centuries in history. The Pope asks, "Does not ... this century ... reveal to a previously unknown degree that manifold subjection to futility?" (n. 8). He cites armed conflicts, dehumanizing industrialization, environmental disasters, the fear of self-destruction brought on by nuclear weapons and the prevalence of abortion as examples of the consequences of man's rejection of God.

Even though we live in an age of space travel and triumphs of science and technology, the world is still "groaning in travail, eagerly waiting for the revelation of the sons of God" (Rom. 8: 19, n. 8). Such "sons of God" are Christians who can transform the world according to the spirit of the Gospel.

The problems of the modern world make us think of the words of the Lord: "Without me, you can do nothing" (Jn. 15: 6, n. 22). Excluding God from the world leads to destruction. After two millennia, the task of implementing the Redemption is still far from complete.

John Paul proclaims the truth of the mystery of the human person when he addresses such questions as: "What is man?" and "What is the source of his dignity and his human rights?" The truth of the mystery of the human person is bound up with the mystery of the Incarnation and the Redemption.

To understand the problems of the modern world and find solutions, we must "make contact with the inward mystery of man" (n. 8). We can do this only by drawing near to Christ the Redeemer. As Vatican II proclaimed, "Only in the mystery of the Incarnate Word does the mystery of man take on light ... Christ reveals man to himself and brings to light his most high calling ... For by his Incarnation, Jesus Christ, in a certain way unites himself with each man..." (n. 8). To understand ourselves, we must know and love Jesus Christ, perfect God and perfect Man. We grow in such knowledge and love especially through prayer, the Gospel and the sacraments.

The Redemption has both divine and human dimensions. It is divine in that it was willed by God the Father as an expression of his eternal love for man. Jesus Christ is the revelation of the mercy of God the Father (n. 9). It is human in that man must respond to the love of God the Father. We must assimilate the reality of the Incarnation and the Redemption in order to understand ourselves. The mission of the Church is to reveal Christ to the world, helping each person to find himself in Christ. To find ourselves, we must first realize our need to love and be loved. "Man cannot live without love" (n. 10).

Redeemed Man and His Situation in the Modern World.

Our relationship with God must be personal. The truth about man demands that each person be able to find Christ "so that Christ may walk with him or her along the path of life" (n. 13). That is, God must be involved in our daily lives. The fundamental task of the Church is to enable this personal union with Christ to take place and to be continually renewed and strengthened throughout one's life.

Every human being on the planet is unique and unrepeatable. Each one is called by God to share in the mystery of Christ (n. 13). If we base our life on Christ's example and cooperate with the grace he has gained for us on the cross, we will become mature human beings. "Mature humanity means [possessing] full use of the gift of freedom received from the Creator when he made man 'in his image, after his likeness'" (n. 21). This gift finds its full realization in unreserved self-giving. Thus, man realizes himself in the gift of self. Self-giving is the source of genuine human flourishing.

Freedom is not an end in itself. "The best use of freedom is charity, which takes concrete form in self-giving and in service" (n. 21). The truth about man is a condition for authentic freedom (n. 12). Freedom cannot be separated from truth.

Each person who has been baptized in Christ has a particular vocation and a unique mission on earth. Lay people are especially called to participate in Christ's kingly mission of ordering the world according to God's plan. This task demands spiritual maturity. "In order to be able to serve others worthily and effectively, we must master ourselves [and] possess the virtues that make this mastery possible" (n. 21). Our dignity as Christians is expressed in our readiness to serve. This is in keeping with the example of Christ who "came not to be served but to serve" (Mt. 20: 28).

In fulfilling our mission, what principles must we follow? The Pope says, "The essential meaning of 'kingship' and 'dominion' of man over the visible world ... consists in the priority of ethics over technology, in the primacy of the person over things, and in the superiority of spirit over matter" (n. 16). Human advancement is not so much a matter of "having more" but rather of "being more" (n. 16). A materialistic, consumerist society condemns man to being a slave to his own products.

The truth about man demands that man work for social justice including solidarity among nations. The world today is a gigantic expression of the parable of Lazarus and the rich man. Such inequality must be overcome (n. 16).

We must work for human rights, especially the right of religious freedom. We must develop a Christian culture in which the truth about man is expressed in law, customs, economics, and morality (n. 17).

The Holy Father ends the encyclical by calling the faithful to persevering prayer so that the present difficulties of the world will become the foundation for "ever more mature achievements on the People of God's march toward the Promised Land" (n. 22).

Dives in Misericordia
(On the Mercy of God).
Encyclical Letter dated November 30, 1980.

In *Dives in Misericordia* Pope John Paul II explains how Jesus Christ reveals God the Father and his merciful love for all human creatures. He maintains that such revelation "constitutes the fundamental content of the messianic message of Christ" (n. 64). The Holy Father discusses the nature of mercy and its relationship to justice. He invites the faithful to meditate on the mercy of God so that they will seek divine mercy and show greater mercy towards others.

The encyclical takes its name from Ephesians 2: 4 where St. Paul says, "God is rich in mercy." What is "mercy?" The Latin word for mercy is *misericordia* which is a combination of *miseri,* meaning pity, and *cordia* which means heart. Thus, *misericordia* is a heartfelt pity, a sympathy in the sorrow of another. Mercy is the dimension of charity that confronts evil: physical, moral or spiritual (n. 79). It especially relates to the evil that one experiences as the result of the actions of another (fn. 52). Mercy enables a person to forgive and be reconciled with a wrongdoer.

The Revelation of God's Mercy.

God's mercy was initially manifested in the Old Testament. When the people of Israel fell into misery because of their sins and infidelities against the covenant, they appealed to God for pardon and received it (n. 27). At the time of the Exodus "the Lord saw the affliction of his people reduced to slavery, heard their cry, knew their sufferings and decided to deliver them" (n. 29). God showed that he is a "God merciful and gracious, slow to anger, and abounding in steadfast love and compassion" (cf., Is. 63: 9, n. 30). Thus mercy is shown to be more powerful than justice and more profound (n. 35). In the final analysis, justice serves love (n. 36).

In the New Testament, the fullness of God's mercy is revealed by Christ. As Jesus says to Philip at the Last Supper, "He who has seen me has seen the Father" (Jn. 14: 9, n. 40). During his public life, Christ made God the Father present among men by the love he bestowed on them. "The blind receive their sight, the lame walk, the dead are raised up, the poor have the good news preached to them" (n. 18). His love was particularly evident when he came in contact with suffering, injustice and poverty (n. 19). By becoming a model of merciful love for others, "Christ proclaims by his actions ... that the call to mercy is one of the essential features of the Gospel *ethos*" (n. 24).

Mercy was also the subject of our Lord's teaching. The story of the prodigal son (Lk. 15: 11-32) expresses the essence of divine mercy. The parable enables us to understand more fully the mystery of mercy in a drama between a father's love and the sins of his son (n. 42).

By leaving home and squandering his inheritance, the prodigal son loses both his material wealth and his dignity as a son. His relationship with his father is ruptured by his foolish actions. Finding himself in desperate need, he decides to go back to his father and appeal to him, not as a son but as an employee (n. 48). To work as a laborer on his father's land will be a humiliation for him, but he knows that this is the most he could deserve as a matter of justice (n. 51).

The father, who is really the main character in the parable, goes beyond the norm of justice. He is faithful to his fatherhood and, having compassion on his son, restores their proper relationship (n. 54). This saves his son's humanity and restores his dignity. It gives the father joy to bring his son back into the family. "He who was dead is alive. He who was lost is found" (Lk. 15: 32, n. 56). The father's behavior shows that the love for a son springs from the very essence of fatherhood and in a way obliges the father to be concerned about his son's dignity (n. 58).

Like the father in the parable, God, who "is love" (1 Jn. 4: 8), is faithful to himself and to his fatherhood (n. 167). His love for man causes him to reach down to a repentant sinner and restore his ultimate good: his relationship with God. In the parable of the prodigal son, we see the possibility of redemption and conversion. "Mercy ... restores to value, promotes and draws good from all forms of evil existing in the world and in man" (n. 63).

Through his passion and death, Christ took on the sins of men and paid the debt they owed to God, thus fulfilling the demands of justice. This work of justice, however, "springs completely from love: from the love of the Father and the Son, and completely bears fruit in love" (n. 72). Thus, the redemption of mankind reveals the perfection of both love and justice. Through the cross, Christ not only renders full justice to God, he also reveals God's merciful love which is stronger than sin and death (n. 81). When we see a crucifix, we should recall the words of St. John's Gospel, "God so loved the world that he sent his only Son ..." (Jn. 3: 16).

The Need for Mercy in Human Relations.

As the result of materialism, the present day mentality tends to exclude the idea of mercy from the human heart (n. 9). The Old Testament attitude of justice based on an "eye for an eye and a tooth for a tooth" (Mt. 5: 38) was challenged by Christ as inadequate (n. 121). The Pope calls such an attitude, which is commonplace today, a distortion of true justice. "The experience of the past and of our own time demonstrates that justice alone is not enough, that it can even lead to the negation and destruction of itself, if that deeper power, which is love, is not allowed to shape human life in its various dimensions" (n. 121). The Church must bear witness to divine mercy by professing it as a truth of faith and seeking to introduce it and make it incarnate in the lives of the faithful and of all people of good will (n. 125).

Each of us is called to practice mercy towards others. "Blessed are the merciful, for they shall obtain mercy" (Mt. 5: 7, n. 139). While strict justice may be applicable in the case of the distribution of material *goods*, mercy must govern human *relationships*. Without mercy, human dignity and brotherhood cannot exist (n. 146). "It is impossible to establish [a] bond between people if they wish to regulate their mutual relationships solely according to the measure of justice" (n. 148). Thus merciful love is indispensable in maintaining proper relationships between husbands and wives, parents and children, friends and neighbors, and co-workers (n. 149).

At the international level, where affairs are mostly governed by strict "justice," the degree of inequality between the rich nations and the poor nations is increasing (n. 114). At the same time a sense of justice is awakening on a vast scale. This is causing increasing international tensions and struggles (n. 117). For there to be true justice among nations, mercy and love must be lived at the international level. The Church ardently desires social justice in today's world and is actively involved in seeking ethical solutions to the world's problems (n. 118).

Forgiveness.

Society can become truly human only when *forgiveness*, which is so much of the essence of the Gospel, is introduced into mutual relationships. "Forgiveness demonstrates the presence in the world of the love which is more powerful than sin. Forgiveness is also the fundamental condition for reconciliation not only in the relationship of God with man, but also in relationships between people" (n. 152). "A world from which forgiveness was eliminated would be nothing but a world of cold and unfeeling justice ...; the various kinds of selfishness latent in man would transform life and human society into a system of oppression of the weak by the strong, or into an arena of permanent strife between one group and another" (n. 153).

As the Pope said on another occasion, "The liberating encounter with forgiveness ... can be experienced even by a wounded heart, thanks to the healing power of love, which has its source in God who is love" (*World Day of Peace Message (1997)*, n. 4). It is easier to forgive others when we remember how much we have been forgiven by God and the price that Christ paid to obtain such forgiveness. We should also remember our Lord's warning, "If you do not forgive others their trespasses, neither will your Father forgive your trespasses" (Mt 6: 15).

The requirement of forgiveness does not cancel out the objective requirements of justice. Forgiveness does not mean indulgence toward evil, scandals, injury or insult. "In any case reparation for evil and scandal, compensation for injury, and satisfaction for insult are conditions for forgiveness" (n. 157).

The Pope ends the encyclical by urging the faithful to have recourse to the fatherly love revealed to us by Christ. We should also pray to Mary, the Mother of Mercy, to join us in imploring God's mercy for humanity in this hour of history (n. 171).

Laborem Exercens
(On Human Work).
Encyclical Letter dated September 14, 1981.

This encyclical commemorates the ninetieth anniversary of *Rerum Novarum*, the great social encyclical of Pope Leo XIII. In *Laborem Exercens*, Pope John Paul II discusses the many dimensions of human work including: work as part of man's *human vocation*, the *requirements* for work to be truly human, the *social aspects* of work and the *redemptive aspects* of work.

The Holy Father says that work is the foundation of the social doctrine of the Church. "[H]uman work is a key, probably the essential key, to the whole social question" (n. 11). "Work" includes paid employment, work in the home and volunteer work.

Human Vocation.

Man was "called" to work even before original sin. Work is a fundamental dimension of man's existence on earth (n. 12). As God said to Adam and Eve, "Be fruitful and multiply; fill the earth and subdue it" (Gen. 3: 19). "Man is the image of God partly through the mandate received from his Creator to subdue, to dominate the earth. In carrying out this mandate, man, every human being, reflects the very action of the Creator of the universe" (n. 13). In other words, human work is in some way a sharing in God's creative power (n. 113).

Man's dominion over the earth is achieved through work (n. 16). It is exercised, for example, in the extraction of natural resources, raising crops, and manufacturing products. "Work is a good thing for man ... because through work man not only transforms nature, he also achieves fulfillment as a human being" (n. 40). Thus, industriousness is an important human virtue (n. 41). One reason why unemployment is so painful is that it leaves unsatisfied an important human need.

Man has a moral obligation to work throughout his life insofar as he is able because the Creator commands it, it is necessary for his ongoing human development, and society needs the fruits of his labor (n. 73). By fulfilling his duty to work, man contributes to the realization in history of the divine plan (n. 115).

We should imitate God not only by working, but also be resting on the seventh day (n. 114). If we do not keep Sunday holy, we risk working with an egotistical motive rather than for love of God and neighbor.

Making Work Truly Human.

The Pope stresses that man should be the *subject* of work, not its *object*. Man must never be treated as a mere tool. Work is for man, not man for work (n. 27). The ethical value of work is determined by its impact on the worker. Does it benefit him and make him a better person? Thus, human work must have a "personal" dimension. Each worker must have some freedom and autonomy so that he can work creatively. He must in some way "be in charge" of his work. A worker must never be treated as merchandise (n. 24). The value of work is not determined primarily by the *kind* of work being done (e.g., manual versus intellectual), but rather by the fact that the one who is doing it is a *person* (n. 26). The error of early capitalism was to treat man as an instrument of production rather than as the effective *subject* of work and its true maker and creator (n. 30).

The Social Aspects of Work.

Work usually constitutes the foundation for the formation of a family. "Thus the family is one of the most important terms of reference for shaping the social and ethical order of human work" (n. 43). If an important purpose of a man's job is to permit him to support a family, it would be an evident disorder if the demands of his job interfered with the fulfillment of his obligations as a husband/father. Similarly, work by a woman outside the home is wrong when it contradicts or hinders the primary goals and responsibilities of the mission of a wife/mother (n. 91).

Work is also the means by which we contribute to the common good of society. All honest work adds to the heritage of the whole human family (n. 44). We should work with a spirit of service with the aim of using our God-given talents to make the world more human and more just.

The Church has always taught the principle of the priority of labor over capital (n. 52). This is really a false dichotomy, however, since capital cannot be separated from labor. Because capital results from labor, the two should not be opposed to one another (nn. 56 and 58). Rather, the fundamental error is "economism" which treats man as merely a material being and ignores his spiritual and religious dimensions (n. 60).

The Church has always upheld the right to private property without treating it as an absolute right (nn. 63-64). Private ownership provides an orderly basis for the development of the goods of the earth for the benefit of all. It also facilitates the "personal" dimension of work: man must have ownership of property to have the autonomy, independence and security required by him and his family. Any socialization of the means of production must insure that each person in some way works "for himself." Failure to do so will result in economic damage and, especially, damage to man (n. 71).

The Redemptive Aspects of Work.

Finally, the Pope discusses human work as a means of sanctification that prepares us for eternal happiness. Jesus Christ was a worker (a carpenter), so we imitate Christ when we work. Our Lord constantly referred to workers in his preaching: shepherds, farmers, fishermen, sowers, doctors, merchants, laborers, etc. (n. 119). Similarly, St. Paul boasted of being a tentmaker and said, "If anyone will not work, let him not eat" (2 Thess. 3: 10, n. 120).

Work must be considered in the light of the cross and Resurrection of Christ. From the time man committed original sin, work has been linked with toil. "By the sweat of your brow you shall earn your bread" (Gen. 3: 17, n. 39). Work is an important means of reparation for sin. It is thus linked to the paschal mystery of Christ. It is an important way of "taking up your cross daily" (Lk. 9: 23, n. 126). We should not run from the cross by putting off our work. "The Christian finds in human work a small part of the cross of Christ and accepts it in the spirit of redemption in which Christ accepted his cross for us" (n. 129). We must see both the indispensability of the cross and the supernatural good that can spring from work when we offer it to God. (n. 129).

The Holy Father concludes the encyclical by urging the faithful to unite their work with prayer so that it will not only contribute to earthly progress but will also extend the Kingdom of God (n. 131).

Dominum et Vivificantem
(Lord and Giver of Life).
Encyclical Letter dated May 18, 1986.

This encyclical on the Holy Spirit follows the encyclicals by Pope John Paul II on Jesus Christ, *Redemptor Hominis*, and on God the Father, *Dives in Misericordia*. *Dominum et Vivificantem* thus completes the series on the Blessed Trinity. The title comes from the Nicene Creed in which the Holy Spirit is professed as the "Lord, the giver of life" (n. 1). The Pope urges the faithful to draw near to the Holy Spirit, the source of eternal life.

Jesus calls the Holy Spirit the "Paraclete," which means "counselor" or "advocate" (Jn. 14: 13, n. 3). The Holy Spirit was sent by God the Father upon the departure of Jesus "in order to continue in the world through the Church, the work of the Good News of salvation" (n. 3). As such, the Holy Spirit "is at the center of the Christian faith and is the source and dynamic power of the Church's renewal" (n. 2). The Holy Spirit is actively involved in the life of the Church and in the lives of its individual members.

The Holy Spirit, the third Person of the Blessed Trinity, is the personification of the love and self-giving between the Father and the Son. "He is Person-Love. He is Person-Gift" (n. 10). The Holy Spirit is sometimes depicted as fire because this expresses the nature of love (n. 41).

The Mission of the Holy Spirit.

As stated by Vatican II, "Having accomplished the work that the Father had entrusted to the Son on earth, on the day of Pentecost the Holy Spirit was sent to sanctify the Church forever so that believers might have access to the Father through Christ in the one Spirit" (n. 25). On the day of Pentecost, when the Church was born, the Holy Spirit came down upon Christ's disciples to remain with them for all time. The Holy Spirit can be said to be the "soul of the Church" because he is its animating principle (n. 26). "The Spirit dwells in the Church and in the hearts of the faithful as in a temple" (n. 25). The primary gifts the faithful receive from the Holy Spirit through the Church are *truth, grace* and *fellowship.*

Jesus calls the Holy Spirit the "Spirit of truth" because he guides the faithful to the truth (Jn. 16: 12, n. 6). "He will teach you all things" (Jn. 14: 26, n. 4). The Holy Spirit guarantees that the Catholic Church will always preserve the truth that the apostles heard from the Master. Through the Church the Gospel will be transmitted to all nations in its integrity for all time (n. 4).

The Holy Spirit transmits divine life to the faithful through the sacraments which "signify and confer grace. ... The Church is the visible dispenser of the sacred signs, while the Holy Spirit acts in them as the invisible dispenser of the life which they signify" (n. 63). The Holy Spirit thus vivifies the faithful by enabling them to participate through grace in the life of the three divine persons. As St. Paul says to the Romans, "God's love has been poured into our hearts through the Holy Spirit" (Rom. 5: 5, n. 10). John Paul calls this outpouring of divine love "God's salvific self-communication" (n. 12).

The Holy Spirit also gives the Church a "unity of fellowship" or solidarity (n. 25). Especially by joining in the celebration of the Eucharist, the baptized make up "one body" which is united in charity (n. 62). The Church is, in the words of Vatican II, "the sacrament of the unity of the whole human race" (n. 64).

Convincing the World of Sin, Righteousness and Judgment.

Jesus said to the apostles at the Last Supper, "I will send the Spirit to you and when he comes, he will convince the world concerning sin and righteousness and judgment" (Jn. 16: 7, n. 27). This passage from St. John's Gospel refers in one sense to the events surrounding our Lord's passion and death. "Sin" means the rejection Christ encountered among his people. "Righteousness" refers to the definitive justice which the Father restored to the Son after his Resurrection and Ascension. "Judgment" means the guilt of the world in condemning Jesus to death (n. 27).

Such "convincing," however, may also be given a broader meaning. It may refer to the salvation of mankind because the Holy Spirit took over from the Son the work of redemption. "Sin" in this sense means the sins of all men because every sin in the history of humanity contributes to the death of Jesus (n. 29). "Righteousness" refers to man's intended salvation in God. "Judgment" means eternal damnation, from which Christ died to save all men (n. 28).

The Holy Spirit "convinces the world concerning sin" by showing the evil that sin contains. Sin is a willful disobedience to God. It is a rejection of the truth of God the Creator (n. 33). Even though man has reason and freedom, he, like all creatures, is subject to limitations. Disobedience means going beyond such limits by trying to be "like God" in deciding for oneself what is good and what is evil. In doing so, man denies that God is the source of moral order in the world (n. 36). Man is prompted to disobey God's law, which is to live a lie, by Satan, the "father of lies" (n. 37).

Conscience.

Man, as the "image and likeness" of his Creator, is called to a life of union with God in truth and love. When man commits serious sin, his relationship with God is ruptured, and he suffers interiorly. By "convincing" man concerning sin, the Holy Spirit "makes man realize his own evil and at the same time directs him toward the good" (n. 42). Conversion of the human heart is brought about through man's conscience which is a gift of the Holy Spirit (n. 36). When man has lost divine grace through sin, the Holy Spirit moves him to repentance and conversion by acting on his conscience.

Vatican II said that man's conscience is at the root of human dignity. It called the conscience "the most sacred core and sanctuary of a man, where he is alone with God, whose voice echoes in his depths" (n. 43). The Holy Father adds, "This capacity to command what is good and forbid what is evil, placed in man by the Creator, is the main characteristic of the personal subject" (n. 43).

The Holy Spirit helps to form and enlighten man's conscience so that it judges whether conduct is good or evil according to the objective standards of morality. Man must purify his conscience so that he can recognize sin. Today, the greatest sin is the loss of the "sense of sin." There is a widespread inability to know the difference between good and evil.

The Pope reminds the faithful that there is a dramatic struggle going on between good and evil, between light and darkness. This struggle is taking place in society and in the heart of each individual (n. 43). As taught by Vatican II, "A monumental struggle against the powers of darkness pervades the whole history of man. The battle was joined from the very origins of the world and will continue until the last day, as the Lord has attested" (n. 44). By relying on the voice of his conscience and by making a valiant effort to correspond to God's grace, man can cling to what is good and be victorious in the struggle against evil (n. 44).

Living in the Spirit.

Man's life is transformed by the gifts and graces he receives from the Holy Spirit. By participating in divine life, man's life acquires a supernatural dimension. Human creatures become, as St. Paul teaches, "children of God" (cf., Rom. 8: 14). Under the influence of the Holy Spirit, man matures and grows strong. He benefits from the gifts of the Spirit: wisdom, understanding, knowledge, counsel, fortitude, piety, and fear of the Lord (n. 15). He can also enjoy the fruits of the Spirit such as "love, joy, peace, patience, kindness, goodness, faithfulness, gentleness, self-control" (Gal. 5: 22, n. 55).

"Man's intimate relationship with God in the Holy Spirit also enables him to understand himself, his own humanity, in a new way" (n. 59). Man learns from Christ that he realizes himself through the sincere gift of self. He is able to practice self-giving in his own life by the power of the Holy Spirit (n. 59).

As more men and women live a life of the Spirit, not only will they be transformed, but God will also permeate the world itself, making it ever more human (n. 59). Ordinary Christians contribute to the "renewal of the face of the earth" when they "put to good use everything that is good, noble, and beautiful in the modern progress of civilization, culture, science, technology, and other areas of thought and human activity" (n. 60). A culture of materialism, on the other hand, which excludes the life of the Spirit, becomes a culture of death and bondage (nn. 56-57).

"When, under the influence of the Paraclete, people discover the divine dimension of their life, both as individuals and as a community, they will free themselves from the bonds of materialism and enjoy the true freedom of the children of God" (n. 60). "Where the Spirit of the Lord is, there is freedom" (2 Cor. 3: 17, n. 60).

The Holy Father urges the faithful to make a commitment to pray often because "prayer through the power of the Holy Spirit becomes the ever more mature expression of the new man, who by means of prayer participates in divine life" (n. 65).

John Paul ends the encyclical by saying, "The Holy Spirit is present and at work: with the breath of divine life, he permeates man's earthly pilgrimage and causes all creation, all history, to flow together to its ultimate end, in the infinite ocean of God" (n. 64).

Redemptoris Mater
(Mother of the Redeemer).
Encyclical Letter dated March 25, 1987.

The publication of *Redemptoris Mater* was the occasion for Pope John Paul II to declare a Marian Year. This period of special devotion to our Lady began on June 7, 1987 (the Solemnity of Pentecost) and ended on August 15, 1988 (the Solemnity of the Assumption) (nn. 49-50). The Marian Year was an important element of the Church's preparation for the Great Jubilee of the Year 2000.

According to tradition, Mary was very young when she gave birth to Jesus. The Church celebrates Mary's birthday on September 8th of each year. Just as the Great Jubilee of the Year 2000 was the celebration of the 2000th anniversary of the birth of Jesus, the Pope wanted a "similar Jubilee in celebration of the birth of Mary" (n. 3). The Marian Year, celebrated 13 years before the Great Jubilee, was intended to mark the 2000th anniversary of Mary's birth. Special indulgences were granted for visiting Marian shrines during this period.

Mary's role in Christianity is unique. "One cannot think of the reality of the Incarnation without referring to Mary, the Mother of the Incarnate Word" (n. 5). Pope Paul VI said, "Knowledge of the true Catholic doctrine regarding the Blessed Virgin Mary will always be a key to the exact knowledge of the mystery of Christ and of the Church" (n. 47).

Mary as the Model of Faith.

Mary is a most special role model for the people of God. "The Church sees in the Virgin Mother of God the most authentic form of perfect imitation of Christ" (n. 47). While Mary lived all of the theological and moral virtues with perfection, she is above all a model of faith. St. Elizabeth said of Mary, "Blessed is she who has believed" (Lk. 1: 45).

At the Annunciation, Mary entrusted herself to God with the full submission of mind and will. Having faith means entrusting "one's whole self freely to God" (n. 13). Faith thus has a moral dimension which involves the will as well as the intellect.

St. Paul calls this complete trust in God "the obedience of faith" (Rom. 16: 26, n. 13). After the Annunciation, Mary devoted herself totally to the person and work of her Son. John Paul describes her life as a "pilgrimage of faith" (n. 14) which at times required heroic obedience to God's will. As predicted by Simeon, who said to Mary, "A sword will pierce you own soul also" (Lk. 2: 34), Mary suffered a great deal to fulfill her mission (n. 16).

Our life is also a journey of faith in which we are called to freely fulfill the unique mission that God has entrusted to each of us. All Christians "in a sense share in Mary's faith" (n. 27). Mary accompanies the people of God on their journey of faith throughout the ages. We seek in her faith support for our own.

Mary's faith is especially visible in the words of the Magnificat (Lk. 1: 46-55) which she expressed at the Visitation. This prayer recalls the words of Hanna, the mother of Samuel (cf., 1 Sam. 2: 1-10) and other passages of the Old Testament. Mary begins the Magnificat with the words, "My soul magnifies the Lord and my spirit rejoices in God my Savior" (Lk. 1: 46). Mary is the first to share in the revelation of the Word made flesh. She is conscious that the promise made "to Abraham and to his posterity forever" (Lk. 1: 55) is being fulfilled in her.

"She is thus aware that concentrated within herself as the mother of [the unborn] Christ is the whole salvific economy" (n. 36). Mary is the first witness of the marvelous truth that "God so loved the world that he sent his only Son" (Jn. 3: 16, n. 37).

Because Mary is totally dependent on God and is completely directed towards him at the side of his Son, she is the most perfect image of freedom and liberation (n. 37). From her we learn that living our faith will make us free.

Mary's Maternal Mediation.

Mary is a mediator but not in the same sense that Christ is. As St. Paul says, "There is one mediator between God and men: the man Jesus Christ" (1 Tim. 2: 5-6). When we refer to Mary's "mediation," we mean her "intercession" (n. 21). As exemplified at the wedding feast at Cana, "Mary places herself between her Son and mankind in the reality of their wants, needs and sufferings ... [S]he can point out to her Son the needs of mankind, and in fact 'has the right' to do so" (n. 21). As stated by Vatican II, "Mary's maternal function towards mankind in no way obscures or diminishes the unique mediation of Christ, but rather shows its power" (n. 38). She is a "mediator" precisely because of her relationship with Christ as his mother.

While Mary's mediation is maternal, it is also virginal. Mary perfectly unites in herself the two ideals of motherhood and virginity. She can both love mankind as a mother and love God as a virgin because her child was God. This permits her to be a perfect cooperator in her son's mission (n. 39). The assumption of Mary into heaven body and soul perfects her indissoluble bond with Christ.

From Mary the Church learns her own motherhood which above all consists in dispensing the sacraments that are the source of divine life for humanity. The Church also learns from Mary how to remain a faithful virgin: to keep whole and pure the treasure entrusted to her as well as to demonstrate total self-giving (n. 43).

Mary as the Mother of Christians.

The essence of motherhood is its concern for the person. "Motherhood always establishes a unique and unrepeatable relationship between two people: between mother and child and between child and mother" (n. 45). A mother has a personal relationship with each of her children because each child is generated in a unique and unrepeatable way.

Mary's motherhood is a gift that Christ himself makes to each one of us. When he said, "Behold your mother" (Jn. 19: 25) on the cross, Christ entrusted humanity to his mother. Just as St. John brought Mary into his home, we have to bring Mary into our home. When we entrust ourselves to Mary, we are directed to Christ. We immediately hear Mary's words, "Do whatever he tells you" (Jn. 2: 5, n. 46).

If Mary is our mother, we should maintain a loving dialogue with her by living some Marian devotions each day. Mary has made it known that praying the Rosary is especially pleasing to her.

The Pope concludes the encyclical by expressing the Church's confidence that Mary, Mother of the Redeemer, will continue "helping the Christian people in the constant struggle between good and evil" (n. 52) in the Third Millennium.

Sollicitudo Rei Socialis
(On Social Concern).
Encyclical Letter dated December 30, 1987.

This encyclical commemorates the twentieth anniversary of *Populorum Progressio (On the Development of Peoples)*, the great social encyclical of Pope Paul VI published in 1967. Pope John Paul II begins the document by affirming that the Church's social doctrine is "directed towards an authentic development of man and society which would respect and promote all the dimensions of the human person" (n. 1). Such dimensions include social, cultural and spiritual, as well as economic (n. 9). The aim of the Church's social teaching is to help the faithful fulfill their duties as responsible builders of earthly society.

The Teaching of *Populorum Progressio*.

Populorum Progressio is a landmark in the development of the Church's social teaching because of its worldwide dimension. Just as Leo XIII in *Rerum Novarum* called for social justice within each country, Paul VI called for social justice among nations. He insisted that the more developed countries have a "most serious duty" to help the developing nations (n. 7). He referred to this moral obligation as the "duty of solidarity" (n. 9).

Paul VI said, "Development is the new name for peace" (n. 10). Peoples excluded from the fair distribution of goods, to which they have a God given right, could be tempted to respond with violence (n. 10). A concern for the common good of all humanity founded on justice, therefore, will contribute to world peace.

Unfortunately, in many ways the situation of the developing countries has worsened since the issuance of Paul's encyclical. The gap is widening between the "developed North" and the "developing South" (n. 14). Instead of a greater "unity of the human race," we are seeing the fragmentation of humanity among a First World, a Second World, a Third World, and even a Fourth World (n. 14).

The economic interdependence of nations, or "globalization" as it is called today, will have disastrous consequences for the weak nations if ethical principles are not applied to international commerce. The poor nations will be taken advantage of by the rich nations, just as laborers were often taken advantage of by the owners of capital during the Industrial Revolution. Therefore, John Paul makes a renewed call for "a true and integral development of individuals and peoples in modern society" (n. 21). This goal can be achieved through the "united cooperation by all for the common good of the human race" (n. 22). It cannot be achieved if the rich nations give in to a "selfish isolation" which would be a "real desertion of a moral obligation" (n. 22).

Some positive signs of development include a greater awareness of human dignity and the need to respect human rights, a growing sense of global interdependence and the need for solidarity, and a greater concern for ecology and the need to conserve natural resources (n. 26).

The True Nature of the Development of Peoples.

John Paul maintains that "the mere accumulation of goods and services, even for the benefit of the majority, is not enough for the realization of human happiness" (n. 28). Nor does technology necessarily bring freedom from every form of slavery. On the contrary, without "an orientation towards the true good of the human race, it easily turns against man to oppress him" (n. 28).

Just as miseries result from underdevelopment, "superdevelopment" can make people slaves of possession and immediate gratification. The sad effect of such "consumerism" in the rich nations is the stifling of spiritual aspirations. "To 'have' objects and goods does not in itself perfect the human subject unless it contributes to the maturing and enrichment of that subject's 'being,' that is to say, unless it contributes to the realization of the human vocation as such" (n. 28).

In today's world, the well to do, who are relatively few in number, often do not realize their humanity because they are hindered by the cult of "having." The very poor, who are relatively numerous, do not realize their humanity because they are deprived of the goods necessary to meet their most basic needs (n. 28). A "full development" of all segments of humanity demands that goods be available to all for use as a *means* to achieve human fulfillment. Goods must not be sought as ends in themselves.

The parable of the talents (Mt. 25: 26-28) is a reminder that Jesus expects everyone to contribute to the full development of others (n. 30). "Collaboration in the development of the whole person and of every human being is in fact a duty of all towards all" (n. 32).

The true elevation of man results from the development of his moral, cultural and spiritual dimensions. "[T]rue development must be based on the love of God and neighbor and must help to promote the relationships between individuals and society. This is the 'civilization of love' of which Paul VI often spoke" (n. 33).

Economic development requires ethical and cultural development because the main obstacles to economic development have a moral character. They include an all-consuming desire for profit and a thirst for power with the intent of imposing one's will on others. Fulfillment of these desires, which are contrary to the will of God, is often sought "at any price" (n. 37).

Solidarity.

Solidarity as a Christian virtue is a combination of justice and charity. It is a "firm and persevering determination to commit oneself to the common good" in recognition of one's responsibility for all (n. 38). Christians must strive to overcome the moral obstacles to development by being committed to the good of one's "neighbor," that is, every human being, with the desire to serve him rather than oppress him. Solidarity requires that all human beings be recognized as persons. Reawakening a religious awareness in individuals and peoples will facilitate this recognition.

Solidarity "is the path to peace and at the same time to development" (n. 39). The motto of Paul VI was *Opus iustitiae pax* (peace is the fruit of justice). John Paul II would say, *"Opus solidaritatis pax"* (peace is the fruit of solidarity), in recognition of the need for *both* justice and charity in achieving world peace.

The Christian faith teaches that one's neighbor is an "image of God the Father, redeemed by the blood of Jesus Christ and placed under the permanent action of the Holy Spirit" (n. 40). As such, one's neighbor must be loved with the same love with which the Lord loves him or her. Such love often requires sacrifice, forgiveness and reconciliation. The unity of the human race ultimately requires a belief in the common fatherhood of God, the brotherhood of all in Christ and the life-giving action of the Holy Spirit. "This supreme model of unity, which is a reflection of the intimate life of God, one God in three persons, is what we Christians mean by the word 'communion'" (n. 40).

True Liberation.

The Holy Father addresses the challenge of "liberation theology" which has appeared in some developing nations and which advocates Marxist solutions to poverty. He says, "Development which is merely economic is incapable of setting man free; on the contrary, it will end by enslaving him further" (n. 46). Development that does not include the transcendent and religious dimensions of man and society is not conducive to authentic liberation. "The principle obstacle to be overcome on the way to authentic liberation is sin and the structures produced by sin as it multiplies and spreads" (n. 46).

John Paul concludes the encyclical by calling on every individual to play his or her part in the campaign for authentic human development. He emphasizes that the pre-eminent role in this task belongs to the laity. "It is their task to animate temporal realities with Christian commitment, by which they show that they are witnesses and agents of peace and justice" (n. 47).

The Pope ends by quoting from the liturgy of the Mass for the Development of Peoples in which the Church prays to the Blessed Trinity: "By sharing the good things you give us, may we secure justice and equality for every human being, an end to all division, and a human society built on love and peace" (n. 49).

Redemptoris Missio
(Mission of the Redeemer).
Encyclical Letter dated December 7, 1990.

In *Redemptoris Missio* Pope John Paul II explains the "why" and the "how" of the Church's mission of spreading the Gospel. He reiterates the urgency of this mission in today's world and invites the Church to renew her missionary commitment (n. 2).

The root words for "apostle" and "missionary" mean "one who has been sent" in Greek and Latin, respectively. They take their origin from Christ's words, "As the Father sent me, so I send you " (Jn. 20: 21) and "Go, therefore, make disciples of all nations ...teaching them to observe all that I have commanded you" (Mt. 28: 19-20, n. 22). Christians are thus "sent" by Christ to spread the Good News. This encyclical is intended to increase the faithful's awareness of this obligation. "No believer in Christ can avoid this supreme duty: to proclaim Christ to all people" (n. 3).

The purpose of apostolic activity is "to serve man by revealing to him the love of God made manifest in Jesus Christ" (n. 2). We serve man when we make Christ known to him because faith in Christ is the greatest gift any man can receive. The Christian faith permits a person to share in the communion that exists between God the Father and God the Son (n. 23).

John Paul exhorts the faithful to undertake the task of evangelization with enthusiasm and optimism. "God is preparing a great springtime for Christianity, and we can already see its first signs" (n. 86). If there is a lack of apostolic spirit, there is a lack of faith. One cannot possess Christ without wanting to share him with others. Furthermore, our own "faith is strengthened when it is given to others" (n. 2).

Although people seem to be sinking deeper into consumerism and materialism, we are also witnessing a desperate search for meaning and genuine spirituality. In secularized societies, the spiritual dimension of life is being sought after as an antidote to dehumanization (n. 38). We must proclaim the divine message to satisfy this spiritual hunger. We should realize that people are much more open to the Christian message than they may appear to be. People are longing for true happiness that can only be found in Jesus Christ. Our salvation is a person, not a set of rules or rituals (cf., n. 18). "Jesus himself is the 'Good News'" (n. 13).

The Pope rejects a false multiculturalism and states that all people have a "right to know the riches of the mystery of Christ" (n. 8). Therefore, we must "open the doors to Christ" (n. 3). "Proclaiming Christ and bearing witness to him, when done in a way that respects consciences, does not violate freedom" (n. 8). Christianity does not reduce freedom. On the contrary, it liberates. "True liberation consists in opening oneself to the love of Christ..." (n. 11).

The Holy Father also rejects "indifferentism," the belief that one religion is as good as another, by showing the impact that receiving the true faith has on a person's life. "The urgency of missionary activity derives from the radical newness of life brought by Christ and lived by his followers" (n. 7). We are freed from the bonds of sin, the grace of the Holy Spirit illuminates our soul and we have access to the fullness of truth about man and his destiny. In drawing near to Christ, we can better understand ourselves. Strengthened by grace, we can also "learn to love, forgive and serve one another" (n. 15).

In the second part of the encyclical John Paul addresses such questions as: What does apostolate consist in? How should lay people participate in the Church's mission? What is God expecting of us? He discusses five means of apostolate: prayer, witness, inculturation, dialogue, and collaboration.

Prayer.

We must realize that we are only instruments or agents of Christ and the Holy Spirit. "The mission of the Church...is God's work" (n. 24). Such mission "is not based on human abilities but rather on the power of the Risen Lord" (n. 23). Therefore, we must first pray and offer sacrifices for those whom we want to evangelize. We should also unite our sufferings to the cross of Christ which will give them redemptive value (n. 78).

Witness.

We must bear witness to Christ in our daily family, social and professional activities. We must strive to grow in the Christian virtues, especially charity, so that we become more Christ-like. "We cannot bear witness to Christ without reflecting his image" (n. 87). If we sin, this will obscure or even deface the image of Christ. We will become obstacles instead of instruments. Spiritual direction will greatly facilitate our ability to bear witness to Christ in our daily life.

Inculturation.

Inculturation refers to making the *world* more Christ-like. It is not enough just to evangelize individuals. Pope Paul VI once said, "[T]he split between the Gospel and culture is undoubtedly the tragedy of our time" (n. 37). John Paul adds, "[T]he field of communications especially confirms this judgment" (n. 37). We particularly need to Christianize the mass media which is so influential in today's "global village" (n. 37).

"Inculturation means the intimate transformation of authentic cultural values through their integration in Christianity" (n. 52). "Since culture is a human creation and is marked by sin, it too needs to be healed, ennobled and perfected" (n. 54). Paul VI specifically stated that the laity must evangelize "politics, society and economics" (n. 72).

Dialogue (or Proclamation).

We must speak to others about Christ and about moral issues. "Each member of the faithful is called to practice dialogue" (n. 57). Lay people, for example, should share their faith with their friends and colleagues. Such "dialogue is based on hope and love, and will bear fruit in the Spirit" (n. 56).

Another way that lay people proclaim the Gospel is by teaching catechism. "Among the laity, catechists have a place of honor" (n. 73). John Paul encourages the laity to undertake this very important activity even though it requires sacrifices.

Collaboration.

We should join with others to more rapidly spread the Gospel (n. 72). We cannot feel alone or isolated as many people do. We should use the resources available to us, for example, the parish and Catholic groups, to be more effective. By working together we can accomplish much more than we could by working separately.

Growing in Apostolic Zeal.

John Paul indicates a number of ways that the faithful can grow in apostolic zeal:

Be more docile to the Holy Spirit. If we strive to grow in spiritual life through prayer and the sacraments, the Holy Spirit can transform us into effective witnesses of Christ and heralds of his word (n. 87). To be better instruments of the Holy Spirit, we must also strive to grow in the Christian virtues, especially humility.

Imitate Christ's spirit of self-sacrifice. As Christ was "obedient unto death, even death on a cross" (Phil. 2: 8, n. 88), we must be willing to sacrifice our time, our comfort and our energy for the salvation of souls. Like the grain of wheat that must die to become fruitful, we must die to ourselves to become apostolically fruitful.

Live the virtue of charity. We must have a burning love for souls inspired by Christ's own charity which was characterized by compassion, availability and interest in the problems of others (n. 89). If we truly love others, we will desire to bring them to Christ. Seeing our charity, others will be drawn to Christ who is the source of our charity.

Love the Church. "Only profound love for the Church can sustain missionary zeal ... Fidelity to Christ cannot be separated from fidelity to the Church" (n. 89). This is because "the Church's fundamental function...is to direct man's gaze...toward the mystery of Christ" (n. 4).

Strive for holiness. Holiness is the fundamental presupposition for doing apostolate. "Let us remember the missionary enthusiasm of the first Christian communities. [Their] proclamation of the Gospel quickly reached the ends of the earth... Underlying this missionary dynamism was the holiness of the first Christians" (n. 90). "You must be like the first Christians and radiate enthusiasm and courage...in generous devotion to God and neighbor. In a word, you must set yourself on the path to holiness. Only thus can you be a sign of God in the world and re-live in your own countries the missionary epic of the early Church" (n. 91).

Just as the first disciples Christianized the Roman world, the Holy Father encourages the faithful to Christianize the modern world. "Christian hope sustains us in committing ourselves fully to the new evangelization and the worldwide mission, and leads us to pray as Jesus taught us: 'Thy Kingdom come, Thy will be done, on earth as it is in heaven'" (Mt. 6: 10, n. 86).

John Paul concludes the encyclical by entrusting to Mary, the Mother of Jesus, all who carry out the Church's missionary mandate (n. 92).

Centesimus Annus
(On the Hundredth Anniversary of Rerum Novarum).
Encyclical Letter dated May 1, 1991.

This encyclical was issued by Pope John Paul II to commemorate the centennial of *Rerum Novarum,* published by Pope Leo XIII in 1891. In *Centesimus Annus* John Paul reflects on the major social developments of the century and addresses the primary social issues facing modern society. He says that the Church will always proclaim social justice because this is an essential part of its evangelizing mission. In doing so, the Church bears witness to Christ the Savior in the life of society (n. 5).

"[T]he guiding principle of Pope Leo's encyclical, and of all the Church's social doctrine, is a correct view of the human person and the person's unique value ... God has imprinted his own image and likeness on human beings, conferring upon them an incomparable dignity" (n. 11). Thus, the foundation of the Church's social doctrine is the dignity which belongs to each man, woman and child as an image of God. Certain fundamental human rights flow from one's essential dignity as a person. The Church is committed to defending and promoting such rights (n. 22).

The Prophetic Teaching of *Rerum Novarum*.

In *Rerum Novarum* Leo XIII proclaimed the fundamental conditions of justice in economic and social life during the social upheaval that followed the Industrial Revolution. He affirmed both the dignity of the worker and the dignity of work as part of the

Encyclicals   37

vocation of every person. "A human being expresses and fulfills himself by working" (n. 6). His proclamation of workers' rights, such as the right to form unions, the right to just wages, the right to work in safe and hygienic conditions, and the right to humane working hours, resulted in a dramatic improvement in the condition of workers.

Pope Leo criticized the two competing social and economic models of his time, Marxist socialism and *laissez-faire* liberalism, which were at opposite ends of the ideological spectrum. He maintained that neither system could bring about social justice which is the foundation of peace in society.

According to nineteenth century liberalism, which was known for its "unbridled capitalism," the government should not intervene in the economic sphere. Pope Leo objected to this position because the poor and defenseless must be cared for and protected by the government (n. 10). "[T]he State has the duty of watching over the common good and of insuring that every sector of social life, not excluding the economic one, contributes to achieving that good, while respecting the rightful autonomy of each sector" (n. 11). The State has the task of determining the proper juridical framework within which economic affairs are to be conducted (n. 15).

Pope Leo also opposed Marxist socialism (also known as "Communism"). He correctly predicted that socialism as a cure for the "worker problem" would be worse than the disease. Marxist socialism must fail because of its erroneous conception of man. John Paul describes its main errors as follows: *It denies man's personal autonomy.* "Socialism considers the individual person simply as an element, a molecule within the social organism so that the good of the individual is completely subordinated to the functioning of the socioeconomic mechanism" (n. 13). *It denies the right to personal property.* Man loses the possibility of personal initiative and becomes wholly dependent on a social machine. *It denies God.* "The denial of God deprives the person of his foundation and consequently leads to a reorganization of the social order without reference to the person's dignity and responsibility" (n. 13). *It denies law* and replaces it with force. Its erroneous view that the end justifies the means leads to such consequences as terrorism and total war. *It denies freedom.* It detaches human freedom from obedience to the truth and consequently from the duty to respect the rights of others.

The collapse of European Communism in 1989 was precipitated by: 1) the violation of the rights of workers by the Communist regimes which was first opposed by the Solidarity movement in Poland (n. 23), 2) the inefficiency of the Communist economic system which reduced the population to poverty and which bred corruption, and, especially, 3) the spiritual void brought about by atheism which led young people to search for personal identity and a meaning of life based on truth and goodness. This search was supported by the witness of those who remained faithful to God during the time of persecution.

Consumerism.

A threat to both Western and post-Communist societies is materialistic consumerism. A consumer society may seek to defeat Marxism on the level of pure materialism, that is, by the ability to produce more goods in a "free" market while equally excluding spiritual values. Such a society, however, would effectively deny the value of morality, law, culture, and religion, and thus, like Marxism, it would reduce man to the sphere of economics and the satisfaction of material needs (n. 19).

Where consumerism takes hold in the life of a person or of a society, material and instinctive dimensions dominate interior and spiritual ones. Freedom is reduced to a self-love consisting of an unbridled affirmation of self interest which refuses to be limited by any demand of justice. (n. 17). Consumerism thus leaves man spiritually impoverished and is an obstacle to his attainment of temporal and eternal happiness.

The Holy Father says, "It is not wrong to want to live better; what is wrong is a style of life which is presumed to be better when it is directed towards 'having' rather than 'being,' and which wants to have more, not in order to be more but in order to spend life in enjoyment as an end in itself. It is, therefore, necessary to create lifestyles in which the quest for truth, beauty, goodness, and communion with others for the sake of common growth are the factors which determine consumer choices, savings and investment" (n. 36).

A consumerist mentality can impede the formation of a family by leading people to "consider themselves and their lives as a series of sensations to be experienced rather than a work to be accomplished" (n. 39). This can result in an inability to make a commitment to marriage and can cause children to be viewed as "things" that one can have or not have according to taste (n. 39).

Alienation.

John Paul explains why materialistic consumerism produces alienation. "[W]hen man is seen more as a producer or consumer of goods than as a subject who produces and consumes in order to live, then economic freedom loses its necessary relationship to the human person and ends up by alienating and oppressing him" (n. 39). Alienation, the loss of authentic meaning of life, occurs in a consumerist society "when people are ensnared in a web of false and superficial gratifications rather than being helped to experience their personhood in an authentic and concrete way." (n. 41).

Materialism ignores man's spiritual and moral dimension which gives him a "capacity for transcendence," that is, an ability to have a spiritual relationship with God and others. "A person is alienated if he refuses to transcend himself and to live the experience of self-giving and of the formation of an authentic human community oriented towards his final destiny, which is God. A society is alienated if its forms of social organization, production and consumption make it more difficult to offer this gift of self and to establish solidarity between people" (n. 41).

The temporal world alone does not answer the mystery of man. It does not explain the meaning of life, the meaning of death, or the meaning of suffering. Man without the transcendent is "alienated" no matter how many material possessions he has (n. 41). What provides fulfillment is the free gift of self to God and others.

The Requirements for Democracy.

Materialism constitutes a threat to democracy because, "if there is no transcendent truth, in obedience of which a person achieves his full identity, then there is no sure principle for guaranteeing just relations between people. Their self-interest as a class, group or nation will inevitably set them in opposition to one another. If one does not acknowledge transcendent truth, then the force of power takes over, and each person tends to make full use of the means at his disposal in order to impose his own interests or his own opinion, with no regard for the rights of others" (n. 44).

"Authentic democracy is possible only in a State ruled by law, and on the basis of a correct conception of the human person. ... [I]f there is no ultimate truth to guide and direct political activity, then ideas and convictions can easily be manipulated for reasons of power. As history demonstrates, a democracy without values easily turns into open or thinly disguised totalitarianism" (n. 46).

A Proper Market Economy.

While the Church does not provide specific technical, economic or political solutions, it does present a Christian vision of the human person which is the basis for a correct picture of society (n. 43).

The political order must take into account the reality of sin. While created for freedom, humankind "bears within itself the wound of original sin which constantly draws persons toward evil and puts them in need of redemption ... The human person tends toward good, but is also capable of evil" (n. 25).

A market economy, within an appropriate juridical framework which is oriented towards the common good, can lead to true economic and civil progress (n. 42). This will be the case if the economic system recognizes the positive role of business, private property and free human creativity in developing the goods of the earth for the benefit of all. The earth will yield its fruits through human work undertaken with intelligence and freedom. "In our time, the role of human work is becoming increasingly important as the productive factor both of nonmaterial and of material wealth" (n. 31).

One's work is usually interrelated with the work of others. In many cases it is undertaken in large business organizations. Workers form a "community of work" when they work towards a common goal in producing goods or providing services (n. 32). In performing disciplined, creative work in close collaboration with others, workers can grow in important virtues such as diligence, industriousness, prudence, reliability, loyalty, and courage (n. 32).

The Pope ends the encyclical by thanking all who study and make known the Church's social teaching (n. 56). He also thanks God who has granted his Church the light and strength to accompany humanity on its earthly journey towards its eternal destiny (n. 62).

Veritatis Splendor
(The Splendor of Truth).
Encyclical Letter dated August 6, 1993.

In *Veritatis Splendor* Pope John Paul II reflects on the Church's moral teaching which is so often distorted or denied in today's world. At the root of today's moral confusion is the separation of human freedom from objective moral truth (n. 4). Such truth should enlighten man's intelligence and shape his freedom. The ultimate aim of morality is to permit man to have ever greater communion with God and with other persons. Unless man lives a morally upright life, he will neither realize his human potential nor be fit for the Kingdom of God.

Topics addressed in this encyclical include the connection between moral good and the fulfillment of man's destiny, the relationship between freedom and God's law, the role of conscience, and the determination of the morality of a human action.

The Connection Between Moral Good and Man's Ultimate Destiny.

The Holy Father begins by referring to the dialogue between Jesus and the rich young man contained in Matthew's Gospel (Mt. 19: 16-21, n. 6). The young man asks our Lord, "What should I do to attain eternal life?" The "question is not so much about rules to be followed, but about the full meaning of life" (n. 7). Christ begins by instructing the yound man to "keep the commandments," thus confirming the Decalogue as "the way and condition of salvation" (n. 12).

The commandments safeguard the dignity of every human being and thus "constitute the indispensable rules of all social life" (n. 97). The negative precepts of the Second Tablet "express with particular force the ever urgent need to protect human life, the communion of persons in marriage, private property, truthfulness and people's good name" (n.13). They preserve man from economic, physical, and moral harm. The commandments are "the first necessary step on the journey toward freedom" (n. 13). Being free of crimes, such as murder, theft and adultery, however, is "only the beginning of freedom, not perfect freedom" as St. Augustine observed (n. 13).

Christ then says to the young man, "If you wish to be perfect, sell your possessions and come follow me" (Mt. 19: 21, n. 16). His answer alludes to the first of the Beatitudes ("Blessed are the poor in spirit for theirs is the kingdom of heaven") contained in the Sermon on the Mount (Mt. 5: 3, n. 16). The Beatitudes (detachment, humility, justice, mercy, purity, etc.) go beyond mere rules of behavior. They speak of basic attitudes and dispositions toward God and neighbor that are associated with personal sanctity. The Pope describes the Beatitudes as a "sort of self-portrait of Christ and for this very reason are invitations to discipleship and to communion of life with Christ" (n. 16).

By referring to the Beatitudes, Christ indicates to the young man that human perfection and eternal life demand possession of the virtues, especially the capacity for self-giving. Self-gift is at the root of the true freedom to which man is called (n. 17). To permit the young man to attain full human maturity, and with it, eternal life, Christ invites him to make a radical gift of himself to God. This would mirror Christ's own gift of himself to man (n. 20). "The crucified Christ reveals the authentic meaning of freedom; he lives it fully in the total gift of himself and calls his disciples to share in his freedom" (n. 85). When man imitates the self-giving of Christ who "laid down his life for his friends" (Jn. 15: 13, n. 20), he achieves his own perfection. In becoming Christ-like, man becomes himself.

Following Christ involves not only accepting the commandments, but also "holding fast to the very person of Jesus, partaking of his life and destiny, sharing in his free and loving obedience to the will of the Father" (n. 19). Man is able to imitate and live out the love of Christ with the assistance of grace received from the Holy Spirit (n. 23).

The vocation to perfect love is not restricted to a small group of individuals (n. 18). All are called to a perfection whose measure is God alone: "You, therefore, must be perfect as your heavenly Father is perfect" (Mt. 5: 48, n. 18).

Freedom and God's Law.

Present day moral issues addressed by the Holy Father include the tension between obedience to God's law and the modern notion of freedom. "Morality" refers to "the good and evil of human acts and of the person who performs them" (n. 29).

In modern thought freedom is often exalted to the point of becoming an absolute. This individualist ethic, however, is inconsistent with man's condition as a creature subject to limitations. The "power to decide what is good and evil does not belong to man, but to God alone" (n. 35).

Authentic freedom consists in choosing the good and living in accordance with the truth of one's nature. There is no conflict between freedom and natural law because such law has God as its author. "God's law does not reduce, much less do away with, human freedom; rather it protects and promotes that freedom" (n. 35).

Genuine freedom is "an outstanding manifestation of the divine image in man ... God willed to leave man in the power of his own counsel, so that he would seek his Creator of his own accord and would freely arrive at full and blessed perfection" united to God (n. 38). Man has the immense dignity of being called to rule himself, as well as the visible world, in accordance with God's will. In submitting to God's law, man freely submits to the truth of creation (n. 41).

Vatican II further explains the true nature of human freedom: "Human dignity requires man to act through conscience and free choice, as motivated and prompted personally from within, and not through blind internal impulse or merely through external pressure. Man achieves such dignity when he frees himself from all subservience to his feelings, and in a free choice of the good, pursues his own end by effectively and assiduously marshalling the appropriate means" (n. 42.) The mature person, therefore, is one who does not act by compulsion or coercion but rather, as master of himself, freely chooses the good and freely acts so as to attain it.

In order to choose the good, however, man must be able to distinguish good from evil. Man is able to do this through the use of his reason which "is the reflection in man of the splendor of God's countenance" (n. 42). Man's natural gift of reason is further enlightened by divine revelation and faith (n. 44).

The Pope confirms Catholic teaching on the distinction between mortal sin and venial sin (n. 70). Mortal sin, whose object is grave matter and which is committed with full knowledge and deliberate consent, takes divine life away from the soul. Mortal sin is not limited to sin committed directly against God because any gravely disordered choice constitutes a rejection of God's love (n. 70). Venial sin weakens the soul and disposes a person to commit mortal sin.

Conscience.

"The relationship between man's freedom and God's law is most deeply lived out in the 'heart' of the person, in his moral conscience" (n. 54). Conscience is "the sanctuary of man, where he is alone with God, whose voice echoes within him" (n. 55). Conscience makes a practical judgment which "makes known what man must do or not do or which assesses an act already performed by him" (n. 59). Its dignity is to discern the truth about moral good and evil as indicated by natural law which is the universal and objective norm of morality.

Like a judge, the conscience does not make the law. Rather it applies the facts to the moral law. The conscience does not liberate, it binds. Man *must* act in accordance with it (n. 60). "[I]t is a *moral judgment about man and his actions*, a judgment either of acquittal or of condemnation, according as human acts are in conformity or not with the law of God written on the heart" (n. 59). We must take care to properly form our conscience in accordance with the truth taught by the Church (n. 64).

Determining the Morality of an Act.

Human acts express and determine the goodness or evil of the individual who performs them (n. 71). They define a person's spiritual traits. Everything we do has an impact on our character for good or bad. "Acting is morally good when the choices of freedom are in conformity with man's true good and thus express the voluntary ordering of the person toward his ultimate end: God himself, the supreme good in whom man finds his full and perfect happiness" (n. 72). The morality of a human act is determined by the object of the act, the intention of the acting person, and the surrounding circumstances. The "object" of the act is the freely chosen kind of behavior (n. 78). As stated in the *Catechism of the Catholic Church,* "There are certain specific kinds of behavior that are always wrong to choose because choosing them involves a disorder of the will, that is, a moral evil" (n. 78). Evil done with a good intention cannot be excused. "You cannot do evil with the hope that good will come from it" (cf., Rom. 3: 8, n. 78). Thus, the end does *not* justify the means. A Christian must be willing to be a martyr rather than do evil (n. 91). To act otherwise would be to compromise the reason for living (n. 96). A Christian must be willing to carry the cross if he is to live a morally upright life.

The Pope ends the encyclical by calling for a new evangelization which must include the proclamation of Christian morality so that society can be filled with the peace and joy that belongs to those who do God's will (n. 107). In this apostolic effort, the witness of a life of holiness will be "the simplest and most attractive way to perceive at once the beauty of truth, the liberating force of God's love, and the value of unconditional fidelity to all the demands of God's law" (n. 107).

Evangelium Vitae
(The Gospel of Life).

Encyclical Letter dated March 25, 1995.

In *Evangelium Vitae* Pope John Paul II proclaims the Good News about human life and provides a vision of hope for humanity's future. The Holy Father discusses present day threats to life, why life is sacred and must be preserved, how the commandment "Thou shalt not kill" applies to current issues, and the necessity of building a new culture of life in society.

Jesus spoke about the heart of his mission when he said, "I came that you may have life and have it abundantly" (Jn. 10: 10, n. 1). By "life" the Lord meant supernatural life consisting of communion with God. Every man is called to this life which begins on earth through grace and which is fully realized in eternity. This is the life by which all aspects and stages of human life take on their true significance (n. 1). Precisely because of man's supernatural calling, human life is sacred from the moment of conception to the moment of natural death. The "Gospel of Life," therefore, is the Good News about man's calling to divine life and the corresponding duty to respect the lives of all, including the lowliest and least gifted.

The purpose of this encyclical is to reaffirm the value of human life and its inviolability and to appeal to everyone to "respect, protect, love and serve life" (n. 5). Only in doing so will mankind find justice, true freedom, peace and happiness.

Present Day Threats to Human Life.

Today there are extraordinary threats to life, especially where life is weak and defenseless. Crimes against life are becoming legal and socially acceptable. The end result is tragic: consciences are being darkened and confused to the point that people cannot distinguish between good and evil.

The roots of violence against life are evident in the Book of Genesis. "Man's revolt against God in the earthly paradise is followed by the deathly combat of man against man" (n. 8). First Adam and Eve rebelled against God, then Cain murdered Abel. From this we learn that, if the link between God and man is broken, the result will be enmity among men.

Because man needs a relationship with God the Father to treat other men as brothers, secular humanism, which excludes God from daily life, necessarily evolves into a culture of death. This is characterized above all by a war of the powerful against the weak. Where acceptance of God is lacking, the law of "might makes right" prevails. Anything can be justified including abortion and euthanasia. Human life becomes just another commodity. Today's crimes against innocent life have fulfilled the prophecy of Jeremiah: "They have filled this place with the blood of the innocents" (Jer. 19: 14, n. 49).

There is a "conspiracy against life" involving governments, international organizations, and the mass media. The latter constantly depict pro-life people as enemies of freedom and progress (n. 17). The policy of some governments to control population growth by force is reminiscent of the ancient pharaoh in Egypt who ordered male Hebrews to be killed (n. 16).

In today's society we hear more than ever about the value and dignity of every individual. At the same time, however, these noble proclamations are repudiated in practice. What explains this remarkable contradiction? The Pope says that personal subjectivity is being carried to such an extreme that each person considers himself to be autonomous and not subject to any objective standard of conduct. People believe that they are free to do whatever they desire and have the power to do. This is an incorrect notion of freedom in which the will of each individual is absolutely exalted and which results in the domination of the strong over the weak (n. 19).

Modern man would answer "no" to Cain's question, "Am I my brother's keeper?" (Gen. 4: 9). The answer should be "yes" because true human freedom comes from service to others. Man attains happiness and fulfillment, not from selfishness, but from the gift of self and openness to his fellow man (n. 19).

The modernist view of freedom has implications for society, especially in a democracy. It causes society to lose a sense of the common good and to become a mass of individuals, each seeking his or her own interest. This undermines democracy and facilitates the establishment of a form of totalitarianism where the most powerful interest groups prevail. If the law is used to trample on the rights of the weak, democracy becomes a caricature, and the democratic state begins to disintegrate because it no longer has legitimacy (n. 20).

As indicated above, the origin of the culture of death is the loss of the sense of God. This results in a practical materialism which breeds individualism, utilitarianism and hedonism. "Quality of life" is seen purely as material well-being (consumerism, pleasure, etc.) with no spiritual or religious dimension. Suffering must be avoided at all costs. People are considered not for what they "are" but for what they "have," "do" or "produce." The first victims of this materialistic mentality are women, children, the sick, the suffering, and the elderly (n. 23).

In the midst of the current state of affairs, however, it should be remembered that the voice of the Lord still echoes in the conscience of every individual. The blood of Abel foreshadowed the blood of Christ. Christ's sacrifice on the cross reveals to man that his greatness consists in the sincere gift of self. It is from the blood of Christ that we must draw the strength to commit ourselves to promoting life. In this dramatic clash between good and evil, between the "culture of life" and the "culture of death," each of us must be unconditionally pro-life. As Moses said, "Choose life, that you and your descendants may live" (Deut. 30: 15-19, n. 25). Each of us must proclaim, celebrate, and serve the Gospel of Life.

The Christian Message Concerning Life.

Human life is sacred and must be protected because man is made in God's "image and likeness" (Gen. 1: 26). Man has an immaterial and immortal soul which God directly creates in each human procreation. In the words of Eve, "I have begotten a man with the help of the Lord" (Gen. 4: 1). Life is thus a gift by which God shares something of himself with his creatures. "Through the act of procreation, a man and woman become partners [with God] in a divine undertaking: God's gift is accepted and a new life opens to the future" (n. 43).

By his death, Jesus proclaimed that life finds its meaning and fulfillment when it is given up (n. 51). We too are called to give our lives by serving others. Each person has a vocation from God that only he or she can fulfill. The premature termination of a person's life would prevent his or her mission from being accomplished.

"Thou Shall Not Kill."

As the giver of life, God is the sole Lord of human life. Man cannot do with it what he wills. Life is entrusted to man as a treasure, and he must render an account of it to his master. The commandment, "Thou shall not kill," reflects life's sacredness and inviolability (n. 39).

The death penalty as a punishment for crime ought not to be applied except in cases of absolute necessity. "Today ... such cases are very rare, if not practically non-existent" (n. 56).

The Pope affirms the Church's condemnation of abortion in unequivocal language: "I confirm that the direct and voluntary killing of an innocent human being is always gravely immoral" (n. 57). "The moral gravity of procured abortion is apparent if we recognize that we are dealing with murder" (n. 58). "The human being is to be respected and treated as a person from the moment of conception" (n. 60).

The Pope also reiterates that euthanasia is a "grave violation of the law of God" (n. 63). To forego extraordinary or disproportionate forms of medical treatment, however, is not euthanasia; rather, it is the acceptance of the human condition in the face of death (n. 65).

The Pope documents the consistent teaching of the Church on abortion and euthanasia for 2,000 years by citing many ancient and modern authorities including the Didache, Tertullian, Popes Pius XI and John XXIII, and Vatican II. For example, he quotes a statement of St. Augustine opposing "assisted suicide" (n. 66).

In a democratic society a politician cannot separate his private conscience from his public conduct. (One cannot be "personally opposed" to abortion and still vote for it.) Democracy as a system depends on conformity to the moral law. If ethical relativism succeeds in replacing the moral law, "the democratic system would be shaken to its foundation" (n. 70). The purpose of civil law is to guarantee an ordered social coexistence in true justice. It must protect fundamental rights, the first of which is the right to life. If this right is lacking, "the sense of justice is lost and mutual trust, the basis of every authentic interpersonal relationship, is undermined at its root" (n. 66).

Promoting a New Culture of Life.

Catholics must be known as "the people of life and for life" (n. 78). As such, we must promote a culture of life as an essential part of our proclamation of the Gospel. This proclamation requires "the presentation of human life as a...gift of God, the fruit and sign of his love. It is the proclamation that Jesus has a unique relationship with every person, which enables us to see in every human face the face of Christ" (n. 81).

To proclaim the Gospel of Life we must first foster a contemplative outlook: we must have a life of prayer linking ourselves with God (n. 83). Then comes action: we must be involved in social and political activities that promote life and be generous in volunteering our time and energy. The "structure of sin" that opposes unborn human life must be dismantled (n. 59). We must commit ourselves to changing unjust laws that permit violence against life. Such laws are not inevitable. As long as they exist, they will be a seed of corruption for society.

We must raise our children as Christians: the witness of Christian families is vitally important in building a new culture of life. Because the trivialization of sexuality is among the principal factors which have led to contempt for a new life, children must be trained in chastity as a virtue which fosters personal maturity and makes one capable of respecting the "spousal" meaning of the body (n. 97).

The Pope provides a special message for women who have had abortions. He encourages them to seek forgiveness from God in the sacrament of reconciliation and to ask forgiveness from their children who are now living with the Lord. They should also become eloquent defenders of life and should care for those in need (n. 99).

The Holy Father concludes the encyclical with a prayer to Mary, the Mother of God, that we may have the strength to build a culture of life and an authentic civilization of truth and love in the Third Millennium.

Ut Unum Sint
(That All May Be One).
Encyclical Letter dated May 25, 1995.

In *Ut Unum Sint* Pope John Paul II renews the Catholic Church's commitment to "re-establish full visible unity among all the baptized" (n. 77). This ecumenical task was one of the pastoral priorities of his pontificate (n. 99). The encyclical takes its name from Christ's prayer for unity among his disciples on the eve of his sacrifice on the cross, "... that they may all be one ... " (Jn. 17: 21, n. 9). Christian unity is not only an ideal to strive for. Catholics must have the conviction that it can be achieved. "Concern for restoring unity pertains to the whole church, faithful and clergy alike. It extends to everyone according to the potential of each" (n. 101). (The movement promoting Christian unity is known as "ecumenism," a term derived from the Greek word for "universal.")

As stated by Vatican II, the division among Christians "openly contradicts the will of Christ, provides a stumbling block to the world and inflicts damage on the most holy cause of proclaiming the good news to every creature" (n. 6). Pope Paul VI said, "The division among Christians is a serious reality which impedes the very work of Christ" (n. 98). John Paul asks, "When nonbelievers meet missionaries who do not agree among themselves ... will they not think the Gospel is a cause of division despite the fact that it is presented as the fundamental law of love?" (n. 99).

"[U]nity, which the Lord has bestowed on his church and in which he wishes to embrace all people, is not something added on, but stands at the very heart of Christ's mission" (n. 9). Unity belongs to the very essence of the community of Christ's disciples. It is an expression of the depth of God's love. The church's unity is constituted by "the bonds of the profession of faith, the sacraments, and hierarchical communion" (n. 9). "To believe in Christ means to desire unity; to desire unity means to desire the church; to desire the church means to desire the communion of grace which corresponds to the Father's plan from all eternity. Such is the meaning of Christ's prayer: 'Ut unum sint'" (n. 9).

While the church of Christ subsists in the Catholic Church, "many elements of sanctification and of truth can be found outside her visible structure. These elements, however, as gifts properly belonging to the church of Christ, possess an inner dynamism toward Catholic unity" (n. 10).

Ecumenism does *not* involve altering the deposit of faith, changing the meaning of dogmas or accommodating truth to the preferences of a particular age. "The unity willed by God can be attained only by the adherence of all to the content of revealed faith in its entirety. In matters of faith, compromise is in contradiction with God, who is truth ... A 'being together' which betrayed the truth would thus be opposed both to the nature of God, who offers his communion, and to the need for truth found in the depths of every human heart" (n. 18).

Personal Conversion and Prayer.

How can Christians be reunited? The ecumenical journey towards unity emphasizes above all the need for interior conversion (n. 15). "Repent and believe in the Gospel" (Mk. 1: 15). "There can be no ecumenism worthy of the name without a change of heart" (n. 15). "Even after many sins which have contributed to our historical divisions, Christian unity is possible, provided that we are humbly conscious of having sinned against unity and are convinced of our need for conversion" (n. 33). "This change of heart and holiness of life, along with public and private prayer for the unity of Christians, should be regarded as the soul of the whole ecumenical movement" (n. 21).

Common prayer with other Christians helps overcome divisions and is an invitation to Christ to join the believers. "Where two or three are gathered together in my name, there I am in the midst of them" (Mt. 18: 20). The Week of Prayer for Christian Unity celebrated January 18-25 has become a widespread and well-established tradition (n. 24). Ecumenical gatherings for prayer provide hope that the union of God's children in truth and charity will some day resemble the union of the divine persons as promised by the prayer of Jesus to the Father: "that all may be one ... as we are one" (Jn. 17: 21-22, n. 26).

Ecumenical Dialogue.

Dialogue with other Christians about matters of faith is more than an exchange of ideas. It is in some way a communication of the person: a gift of self. Ecumenical dialogue will be effective when the participants see themselves as partners in a common quest for the truth (n. 33). "There is a close relationship between prayer and dialogue. Deeper and more conscious prayer makes dialogue more fruitful" (n. 33).

Dialogue must not only be "horizontal, " that is, restricted to meetings, discussions, etc., on the human level. It must also be "vertical," directed to the Redeemer who is the source of reconciliation.

The acknowledgment of sinfulness "creates in brothers and sisters living in communities not in full communion with one another that interior space where Christ, the source of the Church's unity, can effectively act, with all the power of his Spirit, the Paraclete" (n. 35).

Practical Cooperation.

Christians must work together on pastoral, cultural and social projects as witnesses of the Gospel (n. 40). "Through such cooperation all believers in Christ are able to learn easily how they can understand each other better and esteem each other more, and how the road to unity of Christians may be made smooth" (n. 75).

In dealing with other Christians, we must recall the words of Pope Bl. John XXIII: "What unites us is much greater than what divides us" (n. 20).

The change in attitudes that will result from personal conversion, prayer for unity, ecumenical dialogue and practical cooperation will cause increased brotherhood among Christians and greater solidarity in the service to humanity.

Dialogue with the Churches of the East.

Significant progress has been made towards the goal of full communion with the Orthodox Church since Vatican II. Such reunification is necessary for the church to "breathe with her two lungs" (n. 54). In 1965 the mutual excommunications which caused the schism in 1054 were retracted. Pope Paul VI met with the Greek Orthodox Patriarch in Jerusalem in 1964 and in Istanbul in 1967. John Paul II met with him in Istanbul in 1979 and in Rome in 1987. John Paul named Sts. Cyril and Methodius as co-patrons of Europe in 1984 to recognize the role of the Slavic nations in the development of Christian Europe. As the result of the work of a joint theological commission established in 1979, the leaders of the Catholic and Orthodox Churches were able to declare in 1987 that the two Churches profess a "common faith in the mystery of the church and the bond between faith and sacraments" (n. 59).

Just as unity in the church in East and West was maintained during the first millennium of Christianity through the communion of the local bishops with the bishop of Rome, the same structure will permit the re-establishment of such unity (nn. 55-56). Such reunification will accommodate legitimate diversity (n. 57). The church in the West has received many gifts from the East in such areas as liturgy, spirituality, jurisprudence and monasticism.

Dialogue with Post-Reformation Ecclesial Communities.

Common ground with post-Reformation ecclesial communities includes veneration of the sacred Scriptures, the sacrament of baptism, the sense of justice, the importance of fraternal charity and the promotion of peace. Both Pope Paul VI and Pope John Paul II addressed the World Council of Churches in Geneva. John Paul had many ecumenical meetings during his apostolic journeys including one in Columbia, South Carolina, in 1987 (n. 72).

Areas being studied by bilateral theological commissions composed of Catholics and Protestants include: the relationship between sacred Scripture and sacred tradition, the real presence of Christ in the Eucharist, ordination as a sacrament to the threefold ministry of bishop, priest and deacon, the magisterium of the church as entrusted to the pope and the bishops, and the Virgin Mary, as Mother of God and spiritual mother of Christ's disciples (n. 79).

In dealing with non-Catholic Christians, Catholics should be aware of the common heritage of all Christians which includes the witness of the saints and martyrs from all Christian churches and ecclesial communities.

The Ministry of Unity of the Bishop of Rome.

"The Catholic Church is conscious that she has preserved the ministry of the successor of the apostle Peter, the bishop of Rome, whom God established as her 'perpetual and visible principle and foundation of unity'" (n. 88). Pope St. Gregory the Great called the pope the *servus servorum Dei* (servant of the servants of God). The Catholic Church recognizes that the primacy of the bishop of Rome constitutes a difficulty for most other Christians (n. 88).

Such primacy is supported in the New Testament where the person of Peter has an eminent place. "[Y]ou are Peter, and on this rock I will build my church, and the powers of death will not prevail against it" (Mt. 16: 17-18, n. 91). Christ wished to entrust Peter with the task of confirming his brethren in the faith and uniting them in mutual charity. "The ministry of the Successor of Peter is a gift which Christ gave his Bride, so that in every age the unity of the whole People of God would be preserved and fostered" (*General Audience*, August 30, 1995).

The service of unity entrusted to Peter and his successors is not one of exercising power but rather of leading Christ's flock towards peaceful pastures. The mission of the bishop of Rome within the college of bishops consists in "keeping watch" like a sentinel so that the true voice of Christ the Shepherd may be heard in all of the particular churches (n. 94). The "communion of the particular churches with the church of Rome, and of their bishops with the bishop of Rome, is—in God's plan—an essential requisite of full and visible communion" (n. 97).

The Holy Father ends the encyclical by exhorting all of the faithful to pray and work for Christian unity with the confidence that it can be achieved with God's grace because with God nothing is impossible (cf., Lk. 1: 38, n. 102).

Fides et Ratio
(Faith and Reason.)
Encyclical Letter dated September 14, 1998.

"Faith and reason are like two wings on which the human spirit rises to the contemplation of truth; and God has placed in the human heart the desire to know the truth—in a word, to know himself—so that by knowing and loving God, men and women can come to the fullness of the truth about themselves" (n. 1). With these words Pope John Paul II begins *Fides et Ratio,* the first encyclical on the relationship between faith and reason since Pope Leo XIII issued *Aeterni Patris* in 1879.

Shortly after the encyclical was published, John Paul provided his own summary of some of its key elements in an address to a group of U.S. bishops who were visiting Rome. He said that he "wished to defend the capacity of human reason to know the truth. This confidence in reason is an integral part of the Catholic intellectual tradition, but it needs reaffirming today in the face of widespread and doctrinaire doubt about our ability to answer the fundamental questions: Who am I? Where have I come from and where am I going? Why is there evil? What is there after this life?" (*Ad Limina Address* of October 24, 1998, n. 5).

A lack of confidence in one's ability to know the truth has serious consequences for man's behavior in daily life. Without objective truth, man is left adrift (n. 5). Given human weakness and the strength of man's passions, this inevitably leads to tragedy. As the Pope said to the U.S. bishops, "The violent history of this century is due in no small part to the closure of reason to the existence of ultimate and objective truth. The result has been a pervasive skepticism and relativism, which have not led to a more 'mature' humanity but to much despair and irrationality" (*Address*, n. 5).

Truth is known through a *combination* of faith and reason. The absence of either one will diminish man's ability to know himself, the world and God (n. 16). Human reason seeks the truth, but the ultimate truth about the meaning of life cannot be found by reason alone (n. 42).

The Pope first explains the proper roles of faith and reason on man's path to truth. He then explains how they compliment and support one another with complete compatibility.

Faith.

The Church received the ultimate truth about human life as a gift of love from God the Father in the revelation of Jesus Christ. "God so loved the world that he sent his only Son..." (Jn. 3: 16). Christ is the Way, the Truth and the Life (Jn. 14: 6). The true meaning of life, therefore, is a person: Jesus Christ. The truth communicated by Christ is the absolutely valid source of the meaning of human life (n. 12). The ultimate answers to man's questions about pain, suffering of the innocent, and death are found in Christ's Passion, Death and Resurrection (n. 12).

All human creatures, not just philosophers, have the right to receive the truth about their existence and destiny (n. 38). By the revelation of Jesus Christ, God has made the truth accessible to every man and woman. Jesus Christ is not only the revelation of God to man, he is also the revelation of man to himself. In the mystery of the Incarnate Word, man can understand himself. Christ "reveals man to himself and makes clear his supreme calling, which is to share in the divine mystery of the life of the Trinity" (n. 13). Man shares in this mystery on earth through grace and in heaven by direct contemplation of God.

Faith is man's obedient response to God's revelation (n. 13). By faith man accepts the truth of Christ's revelation which is guaranteed by God. Because an act of faith involves freely entrusting oneself to God and freely assenting to His revelation, it has a moral dimension. Preceded by the gift of grace and assisted by the Holy Spirit, it is an act of both the mind and the will. "Men and women can accomplish no more important act in their lives than the act of faith; it is here that freedom reaches the certainty of truth and chooses to live in that truth" (n. 13).

Reason.

Man can know that God exists by reflecting on creation. As we read in the Book of Wisdom, "From the greatness and beauty of created things comes a corresponding perception of their Creator" (Wis. 13: 5, cf., Rom. 1: 20, n. 19). "If human beings fail to recognize God as the creator of all, it is not because they lack the means to, but because their free will and their sinfulness place an impediment in the way" (n. 19).

Man's intellectual capacity, his ability to reason and to think in abstract terms, is a great gift. Man can acquire true knowledge about himself, God and the world. Man is born with a desire to know the truth about himself. It is essential the he find the truth because only by choosing true values by which to live can he be true to his nature and find happiness (n. 25). No one can avoid the need to address life's ultimate questions (n. 27). In fact man can be defined as "the one who seeks the truth" (n. 28). Man must depend to a great extent on others as his source of knowledge. He is unable to factually verify even a small part of his knowledge himself. Therefore, he must trust in the veracity of those who teach him. "This means that the human being – the one who seeks the truth – is also the one who lives by belief" (n. 31).

Belief involves interpersonal relationships because it brings into play not only the capacity to *know* but also the capacity to *entrust* oneself to others. "Knowledge through belief, grounded as it is on trust between persons, is linked to the truth: in the act of believing men and women entrust themselves to the truth which the other declares to them" (n. 32). Martyrs are particularly trustworthy witnesses to the truth about human existence.

The search for the truth about the meaning of life can reach its end only in reaching the absolute because the finite world does not provide a satisfactory answer. Man must not only exercise his reason, he must also trust other persons in the search for ultimate truth. He experiences not only an innate need for the *truth* but also an innate need for a *person* to whom he might entrust himself on the journey to find it (n. 33).

At this point the Christian faith comes to meet him, offering the concrete possibility of reaching the goal he seeks. It enables him to encounter the mystery of Christ (n. 33). Jesus Christ is both the Truth that he is seeking and the Person to whom he can confidently entrust himself to find it. The unity of truth, natural and revealed, is embodied in a living and personal way in Christ. What human reason seeks so ardently can be found only in Christ (n. 34).

With the gift of grace and man's personal assent to God's revelation, the human wisdom known by belief is transformed by theological faith. Thus, in knowing and loving God through faith, man comes to the ultimate truth about himself (n. 1).

The Interaction between Faith and Reason.

The Holy Father next explains the proper interaction between faith and reason and between philosophy and theology. Philosophy is the study of ultimate truth under the natural light of reason. Theology is the study of the Catholic faith with revelation as its first principles. The purpose of theology is to permit a greater understanding of the faith so that it can be grasped more firmly (n. 93).

Reason supports faith and philosophy supports theology in the following ways:

1. Reason prepares the way to faith. St. Justin and the apologists used philosophy as a "preamble" to the faith (n. 38). Philosophical logic shows how the Catholic faith is not contrary to reason, and it can demonstrate the errors of arguments against the faith. Thus, St. Clement of Alexandria called philosophy a "stepping stone to the faith" (n. 38).

2. Reason can show that that there is a God and can demonstrate his primary attributes such as his power and divinity. Reason lays the foundation for faith and makes revelation "credible." Reason is thus the common ground between believers and unbelievers.

3. Faith without reason withers into myth or superstition. Deprived of reason, faith is left with only feelings and experience. It loses its universality (n. 48).

4. Philosophy provides a language for theology. Its concepts and patterns of thought permit theology to have a logical structure and to be a true science (n. 65). For example, while the Real Presence in the Holy Eucharist is to be believed as a matter of faith, theology attempts to make it more understandable in terms of substance, accidents, transubstantiation, etc. Philosophical language permits theology to speak about God, the personal relations within the Trinity, God's creative activity in the world, the relationship between man and God, and Christ's identity as true God and true Man, to take a few examples (n. 66).

John Paul also explains how faith supports reason and how theology supports philosophy:

1. Human reason is inherently weak and inclined to error. Deprived of revelation, reason can go off course and miss its destination (n. 48). Faith warns reason against the paths that will lead it astray (n. 73). It shines light on the true paths (n. 79).
2. Faith stirs reason to explore paths that it would not otherwise have suspected it could take (n. 56). It proposes truths that might never have been discovered by unaided reason. For example, the notions of free will and a personal God who is the Creator of the world have been crucial for the development of a philosophy of being. The Christian proclamation of human dignity, equality and freedom is reflected in modern philosophical thought (n. 76).

3. Faith gives the philosopher the courage to tackle difficult questions such as the problem of evil and suffering, the personal nature of God and the metaphysical question "Why is there something rather than nothing?" (n. 76). His faith gives him the conviction that his reason will find solutions, much as a trustworthy map gives one looking for buried treasure the confidence to keep digging.
4. Faith and spiritual life protect the philosopher from intellectual pride that would impede his ability to search for the truth. Faith, strengthened by love, facilitates the intellectual grasp of the truth about man and his real needs (n. 76).

The Holy Father thus confirms the harmony between the knowledge of faith and the knowledge of reason. "Faith asks that its object be understood with the help of reason; and at the summit of its searching, reason acknowledges that it cannot do without what faith presents" (n. 42). As St. Thomas Aquinas argued, because the light of reason and the light of faith both come from God, there can be no contradiction between them (n. 43).

With the rise of rationalism, faith and reason became separated with disastrous consequences. The end result is the nihilism that we are now experiencing. Nihilism contains no hope of meaning and admits of no objective truth (n. 46). It recognizes only the utilitarian ends of power and pleasure (n. 47). Men and women are treated as objects to be manipulated rather than as persons to be honored. Nihilism is reflected in contemporary culture, for example, in art, music, literature and entertainment. As the result of increasing nihilism, a culture of death is replacing a culture of life. If this continues, the Pope told the U.S. bishops, the next millennium will bring "a new era a barbarism rather than a springtime of hope" (*Address,* n. 3).

John Paul concludes the encyclical by providing challenges for philosophers and theologians. He states that philosophy needs to regain its sapiential dimension, that is, it must renew its search for wisdom and the ultimate meaning of life. Philosophy must transcend empirical data and consider spiritual realities such as truth, beauty, and universal moral values (n. 83). Theology must serve the proclamation of the Gospel in language that can be understood by modern man.

The Holy Father ends by expressing his hope that Mary, Seat of Wisdom, may assist all who devote their lives to the search for wisdom. "May their journey into wisdom, sure and final goal of all true knowledge, be freed of every hindrance by the intercession of the one who, in giving birth to the Truth and treasuring it in her heart, has shared it forever with all the world" (n. 108).

Ecclesia de Eucharistia
(The Eucharist in its Relationship to the Church).
Encyclical Letter dated April 17, 2003.

"The Church draws her life from the Eucharist" (n. 1). Thus begins this encyclical by Pope John Paul II on the Holy Eucharist which was issued on Holy Thursday in the twenty-fifth year of his pontificate. Its purpose is to affirm the Church's doctrine and practice regarding the Eucharist so that it "will continue to shine forth in all its radiant mystery" (n. 10). This sacrament is the Church's most precious possession because it is Christ himself (n. 9). With deep emotion, the Holy Father gives his own testimony of faith in the Real Presence of Christ in the Eucharist, and he thanks the Lord for this gift to the Church (n. 59). He urges the faithful to experience anew the nourishment of the "living bread" that comes down from heaven (n. 7).

The Mystery of Faith.

Christ is present in the Holy Eucharist in the fullest sense. As stated by the Council of Trent, "The consecration of the bread and wine effects the change of the whole substance of the bread into the substance of the body of Christ our Lord, and the whole substance of the wine into the substance of his blood. And the holy Catholic Church has fittingly and properly called this change transubstantiation" (n. 15). The Eucharist is a "mystery of faith" that surpasses our understanding and can only be received in faith (n. 15). Referring to the words of the Eucharistic hymn *Adoro Te Devote*, the Holy Father says, "Here our senses fail us ... yet faith alone, rooted in the word of Christ handed down to us by the Apostles, is sufficient for us" (n. 59).

The Eucharist is not only a reminder of the Lord's passion and death, it is its sacramental re-presentation. "It is the sacrifice of the Cross perpetuated down the ages" (n. 11). When the Church celebrates the Eucharist, this central event of our salvation becomes really present and "the work of our redemption is carried out" (n. 11). Thus, in the Mass each member of the faithful can take part in the events of Christ's redemption and gain their inexhaustible fruits. In the Eucharist Jesus "shows us a love that knows no measure" (n. 11).

In saying, "This is my body which is given for you," (Lk. 22: 19), Jesus expressed the sacrificial meaning of the Eucharist. At the Last Supper he "made sacramentally present his sacrifice which would soon be offered on the Cross for the salvation of all" (n. 12). The Eucharist is a sacrifice in the strict sense. It is first and foremost Christ's offering of his life as a gift to the Father. In taking part in the Sacrifice of the Mass, the faithful "offer the divine victim to God, and offer themselves along with it" (n. 13).

"The Eucharistic Sacrifice makes present not only the mystery of the Savior's passion and death, but also the mystery of the resurrection which crowned his sacrifice" (n. 14). The Eucharist thus points to our future resurrection. It is "in some way the anticipation of heaven, the 'pledge of future glory'" (n. 18). Our Lord said, "He who eats my flesh and drinks my blood has eternal life and I will raise him up on the last day" (Jn. 6: 54, n. 18). The eschatological meaning of the Eucharist should move the faithful to increase their sense of responsibility as Christians to transform their lives and build a more human world — one which is fully in harmony with the Gospel message (n. 20).

The Eucharist Builds the Church.

The Eucharist has been at the center of the Church's growth since its beginning (n. 21). In addition to being a sacrifice, the *"Eucharist is a true banquet* in which Christ offers himself as our nourishment" (n. 16). "My flesh is food indeed, and my blood is drink indeed" (Jn. 6: 55, n. 16). "From the perpetuation of the sacrifice of the Cross and her communion with the body and blood of Christ in the Eucharist, the Church draws the spiritual power needed to carry out her mission" (n. 22). The Eucharist is thus *"the source* and *the summit* of all evangelization since its goal is the communion of mankind with Christ and in him with the Father and the Holy Spirit" (n. 22).

When we go to communion, not only do we receive Christ but Christ also receives us and enters into friendship with us (n. 22). When Mary conceived the Son of God in the physical reality of his body and blood, she anticipated "within herself what to some degree happens sacramentally in every believer who receives, under the signs of bread and wine, the Lord's body and blood" (n. 55). Just as Mary became in some way a living tabernacle when she carried Jesus in her womb, the faithful also bear the body of Christ within themselves for some moments after communion. The communicant should make this a time of intimate dialogue with Jesus as friend (n. 61).

Because Christ remains truly present in the tabernacle under the sacred species after Mass, the Eucharist should also be worshipped outside of the Mass. Daily prayer in silent adoration before the Blessed

Sacrament is an inexhaustible source of holiness (n. 10). In this way we can relive the experience of St. John the Apostle who rested on the breast of the Master (n. 25). If the program which the Holy Father prescribes for the Church as it enters the Third Millennium can be summarized as "contemplating the face of Christ," it consists above all in contemplating the "Eucharistic face" of Christ in the living sacrament of his body and blood (n. 6).

Eucharist piety is also expressed in exposition of the Blessed Sacrament, Eucharistic processions and visits to the Blessed Sacrament. As stated by Pope Paul VI, such visits are a "sign of gratitude, an expression of love and an acknowledgment of the Lord's presence" (fn. 49). All of the expressions of Eucharist devotion are "of inestimable value for the life of the Church" (n. 25). St. Theresa of Avila and other saints recommended cultivating a constant desire for the sacrament of the Eucharist by making "spiritual communions" throughout the day (n. 34).

The Eucharist expresses the apostolicity of the Church because it must be celebrated by a priest whose ordination can be traced through episcopal succession back to the Apostles (n. 29). The Eucharist must always be at the "center and root" of a priest's life and ministry (n. 31). He must not lose this focus in the midst of the many other demands on his time.

The Eucharist and Ecclesial Communion.

The Eucharistic Sacrifice is intrinsically directed towards promoting communion with God and among the faithful (n. 16). The Eucharist perfects our union with God because by it "we attain God and God joins himself to us in the most perfect union"

(n. 34). The Eucharist fosters communion among the faithful because it "superabundantly fulfills the yearning for fraternal unity deeply rooted in the human heart" (n. 24). When the faithful are nourished by Christ's body and blood, they become "one body, one spirit in Christ" (n. 17). The unity of the faithful in the one Body of Christ is promoted by participation in Sunday Mass which Catholics have the obligation to attend unless they are seriously impeded (n. 41).

A person must be in the state of grace to receive the Eucharist worthily because sacramental communion presupposes the *invisible unity of the person with God*. As indicated in the *Catechism of the Catholic Church*, "Anyone conscious of a grave sin must receive the sacrament of Reconciliation before coming to communion" (n. 36).

Access to sacramental communion also presupposes the *visible unity of the person with the Church*. This consists in an acceptance of the Church's faith, sacraments and ecclesial government. Where such bonds of unity are absent, receiving communion would be a contradiction because the unity that the sacrament signifies would not be real. It will thus not be possible to concelebrate the Eucharist with members of the post-Reformation ecclesial communities until such bonds are fully established (n. 44). Neither is it possible to give communion to a person who is not baptized or who rejects the full truth of the faith regarding the Eucharistic mystery (n. 38). Similarly, Catholics must not receive communion distributed in services of the post-Reformation ecclesial communities (n. 46).

The Dignity of the Eucharistic Celebration.

Just as Mary the sister of Lazarus anointed Jesus with costly ointment in Bethany (cf., Mt. 26: 8), the

Church has always devoted the best of her resources to expressing her wonder and adoration before the "unsurpassable gift of the Eucharist" (nn. 47-48). She has always felt the need to celebrate the Eucharist "in a setting worthy of so great a mystery" (n. 48). This sense of mystery has found expression in the Eucharistic Liturgy and in church architecture, sculpture, painting, and music (n. 49). The rich artistic heritage that has developed over the centuries is a genuine service to the faith (n. 50).

Ecclesiastical norms regulating the celebration of the Eucharist and the construction and decor of sacred buildings must be observed with great fidelity (nn. 50 and 52). Unauthorized innovations in the Liturgy, as if it were someone's private property instead of being the heritage of the whole Church, are not acceptable (n. 52).

The Holy Father concludes the encyclical by reiterating that "every commitment to holiness, every activity aimed at carrying out the Church's mission, every work of pastoral planning, must draw the strength it needs from the Eucharistic mystery and in turn be directed to the mystery as its culmination" (n. 60). He urges the faithful to be ever vigilant in guarding the treasure of the Eucharist and to hand it on to future generations of Christians in all of its integrity (n. 61).

Finally, John Paul calls on Mary, "woman of the Eucharist," to help us experience the transforming power of the Eucharist which will enable us to become witnesses of hope in today's world (62).

Catechesi Tradendae
(On Catechesis in Our Time).
Apostolic Exhortation dated
October 16, 1979.

This apostolic exhortation, issued by Pope John Paul II on the first anniversary of his election to the papacy, followed the 1977 Synod of Bishops on catechesis. John Paul had participated in the Synod as the Archbishop of Cracow. "Catechesis" is a Greek word for "teaching." It has come to refer to the Church's efforts to educate people in the life of Jesus Christ so that they may believe that he is the Son of God and share his life in grace and virtue (n. 1). In carrying out the task of catechesis, the Church obeys the words of Christ, "Go, therefore, make disciples of all nations, teaching them to observe all that I have commanded you" (Mt. 28: 19, n. 1).

Catechesis in the Church's Pastoral and Missionary Activity.

The object of catechesis is the mystery of Christ in all of its dimensions. Its purpose is not only to teach the meaning of Christ's works and deeds but also to permit personal communion with him (n. 5). Deeper knowledge of Christian doctrine helps people to entrust themselves to the mystery of Christ and to put their faith into practice (n. 20). Catechists transmit the life and teaching of Jesus by their personal witness of faith as well as by the doctrine they expound (n. 6). The Holy Father says, "The most valuable gift that the Church can offer to the bewildered and restless world of our time is to form within it Christians who are confirmed in what is essential and who are humbly joyful in their faith" (n. 61).

Jesus was properly addressed as "Teacher" during his public life. "You call me Teacher and Lord; and you are right, for so I am" (Jn. 13: 13-14, n. 8). Just as Jesus taught the Good News, the Church carries on this mission as "Mother and Teacher" of all men (n. 11).

Over the course of its history the Church has gained vast experience in the task of catechesis. The Pope summarizes some of the main lessons it has learned. *First,* giving catechesis is a sacred duty and an inalienable right of the Church that must be exercised by her children at all times and in all places. It is an aspect of religious freedom which is a fundamental human right. Unfortunately, this right is being violated in many countries today (n. 14). *Second,* catechesis must be given the highest priority among the Church's good works since it is the foundation of her life as a community of believers. The Church must assign her best people to this task and spare no effort to maximize its effectiveness (n. 15). *Third,* the whole Church must feel responsible for the task of catechesis. Pastors, parents, teachers and all of the faithful must in some way be involved in giving or receiving catechesis (nn. 16 and 45). *Fourth,* catechesis needs to be continually renewed by the utilization of new means of transmitting and expressing the Gospel message. Confusing improvisations, however, must be avoided (n. 17).

"[C]atechesis is the education of children, young people and adults in the faith ... in an organized and systematic way, with a view to initiating the hearers in the fullness of Christian life" (n. 18). Its elements include: the initial proclamation of the Gospel to arouse faith, "apologetics" or the examination of the reasons for belief, the experience of Christian living, the celebration of the sacraments, and giving apostolic witness (n. 18).

Learning Catholic doctrine and growing in spiritual life must go hand in hand. Sacramental life will turn into hollow ritualism if it is not based on knowledge of the meaning of the sacraments. On the other hand, catechesis can become a merely intellectual exercise if it is not integrated with sacramental practice, a life of piety and growth in virtue (n. 23). Without catechesis, not only would one's faith remain immature, one would not be able to defend one's faith in the world (n. 25).

The Whole of the Good News Drawn From its Source.

The primary sources of the Catholic faith are the Creed, the seven sacraments, the Ten Commandments and the Lord's Prayer. (The *Catechism of the Catholic Church*, published in 1992, is organized according to these main headings.) Catechesis must include education in the Christian virtues that are the foundation of personal freedom as well as fraternity, justice and peace in society. The social consequences of the demands of the Gospel must always be taught (n. 29).

Regarding the *content* of catechesis, the Holy Father comments on three aspects that deserve special attention. The first concerns the *integrity* of the content. Because Christ told the apostles to teach "all" that he commanded, it is essential to transmit the faith whole and entire. A catechist cannot pick and choose on the basis of what he considers important or unimportant (n. 30). Second, the *hierarchical* character of its content must be respected. The most important aspects of the faith should receive the most attention (n. 31). Third, catechesis must have an *ecumenical* character. It must reach out to all, especially to other Christians, and reflect the Church's desire for unity (n. 32). This ecumenical dimension will be authentic if it affirms the Catholic identity of the members of the Church while respecting the beliefs of non-Catholics.

Catechesis is imparted in different ways to different age groups. Small children receive the first elements of catechesis from their parents, including learning short prayers (n. 36). The religious instruction of children in elementary school should give meaning to the sacraments and communicate the joy of being a witness of Christ (n. 37). The catechesis of adolescents must address their search for self-discovery and reveal Jesus Christ as a friend, guide and model (n. 38). Young adults must be assisted in growing in maturity and meeting the important commitments of adult life (n. 39). "From infancy until the threshold of maturity, catechesis is thus a permanent school of the faith and follows the major stages of life, like a beacon lighting the path of the child, the adolescent, and the young person" (n. 39).

Ways and Means of Catechesis.

An important means of catechesis is the homily for Sunday and feast day Masses which "should always be carefully prepared, rich in substance, adapted to the hearer, and reserved to the ordained ministers" (n. 48).

Catechesis, as well as evangelization in general, "is called to bring the power of the Gospel into the very heart of culture" (n. 53). The Gospel must transform and regenerate a culture by rectifying many of its elements. Changing the Gospel message to conform to a particular culture, on the other hand, would amount to "emptying the cross of Christ of its power" (1 Cor. 1: 17, n. 53).

There are many possible methods of catechesis. While memorization should not be overdone, there is a real need for Christians to memorize some important Bible passages, the Ten Commandments, the Creed, essential prayers, and certain key doctrinal ideas (n. 55).

The Holy Father urges *bishops* to maintain a passion for catechesis in their dioceses and to provide it with all of the necessary resources (n. 63). He urges *priests* to conduct well-organized catechetical programs in their parishes, reminding them that believers have a right to receive catechesis and that the pastors have a duty to provide it. He thanks *lay teachers* of catechism for their ardent and generous zeal in carrying out this "eminent form of the lay apostolate" (n. 66).

The primary setting for catechesis must continue to be the parish community. Instruction received by children in the parish, however, must be reinforced at home. "Christian parents must strive to follow and repeat, within the setting of family life, the more methodical teaching received elsewhere. The fact that these truths about the main questions of faith and Christian living are repeated within a family setting impregnated with love and respect will often make it possible to influence the children in a decisive way for life" (n. 68).

The Pope ends the apostolic exhortation by turning to the Holy Spirit whose mission is to transform the faithful into true witnesses of Christ (n. 72).

Catechesis is ultimately a work of the Holy Spirit, "a work that he alone can initiate and sustain in the Church" (n. 72). Catechists, therefore, must be aware of acting as instruments of the Holy Spirit.

They must pray that he make their efforts supernaturally effective. They must also seek ever-greater communion with him in order to be docile to his inspirations. A "renewal in the Spirit" can bring about a dynamic catechetical awaking that will lead "the greatest possible number of faithful to make a humble, patient and persevering effort to know the mystery of Christ better and better, and bear witness to it" (n. 72).

The Holy Father also turns to Mary who is "a living catechism" and "the mother and model of catechists" (n. 72). "May the presence of the Holy Spirit, through the prayers of Mary, grant the Church unprecedented enthusiasm in the catechetical work that is essential for her. Thus she will effectively carry out ... the mission given her by the Teacher, 'Go, therefore, make disciples of all nations'" (n. 72).

Familiaris Consortio
(The Christian Family).
Apostolic Exhortation dated November 22, 1981.

Marriage and the family was the subject of the 1980 Synod of Bishops. In this post-synodal apostolic exhortation Pope John Paul II reflects on the family and its role in the realization of God's plan in history. He maintains that the well being of society is intimately tied to the good of the family (n. 3). "The future of humanity passes by way of the family" (n. 86).

Because God is love and man is made in the image of God, it follows that love is "the fundamental and innate vocation of every human being" (n. 11). Marriage is one of the specific ways recognized by Christian revelation of realizing the vocation of the human person to love. In God's plan the family has been established as "an intimate community of life and love" (n. 17). "[T]he family has the mission to guard, reveal and communicate love, and this is a living reflection of and a real sharing in God's love for humanity and the love of Christ the Lord for the Church, his bride" (n. 17)

Marriage is an institution of divine origin. God's design for marriage has been "imprinted on the humanity of man and woman since their creation" (n. 13). The sacrament of matrimony is the "specific source and original means of sanctification for Christian married couples and families" (n. 56). With the assistance of the Holy Spirit, the Church authentically teaches the truth about marriage.

The Church has always taught that marriage has four unchangeable characteristics: *indissolubility, exclusivity, fidelity, and fecundity.*

- It is *indissoluble.* A valid marriage lasts until death. "As a mutual gift of two persons, this intimate union, as well as the good of children, imposes total fidelity on the spouses and argues for an unbreakable oneness between them" (n. 20).

- It is *exclusive.* A marriage consists of one man and one woman. Because marriage requires total self-giving, it cannot be shared.

- It is *faithful.* It admits of no sexual relations outside the marriage. "Total physical self-giving would be a lie if it were not the sign of total personal self-giving" (n. 11). There must be a correspondence between the language of the body and the intentions of the mind.

- It is *fecund or fruitful.* Sexual relations in marriage must be open to life. The two dimensions of the conjugal union, unitive and procreative, must not be artificially separated since this would be inconsistent with the total self-giving demanded by the marital covenant (n. 32).

While all love is a manifestation of self-giving, "conjugal love makes one capable of the greatest gift: the gift by which the parents become cooperators with God in giving life to a new human person" (n. 14). The husband and wife participate with God in the procreation of new human life. At the moment of conception, God creates a new immaterial soul that will last forever. Because procreation is the occasion for direct divine creation, it demands the protection of a strong institution.

The spouses participate in a real way in divine love through their conjugal love. God in a way transmits his love to the man and woman through their experience of marriage. The parents in turn transmit this divine love on to their children when they love them. Parental love becomes for the children "the visible sign of the very love of God" (n. 14).

What does the family need to do to "become what it is" (cf., n. 17), that is, to realize its full potential? The Holy Father discusses the four main tasks of the family emphasized during the Synod: forming a community of persons, serving life, participating in the development of society, and sharing in the evangelization of the world.

Forming a Community of Persons.

In his first encyclical, *Redemptor Hominis,* John Paul said, "Man cannot live without love. He remains a being that is incomprehensible to himself; his life is senseless if love is not revealed to him, if he does not experience love and make it his own" (n. 18). Love is above all a sincere gift of self. What most moves us to love is knowing that we are loved. It is precisely in the family where we learn how to love. Marriage is a school of love. "Honor thy father and thy mother" means that each member of the family should honor the others for their own sake.

Family communion requires a spirit of sacrifice and forgiving. The Pope acknowledges that every marriage is to some extent marred by selfishness. This has to be minimized through personal effort. There is no love without sacrifice (n. 21).

The husband and the wife have equal dignity. "The mentality which honors women more for their work outside the home than for their work within the family must be overcome" (n. 23). A special task of the father is to ensure the harmonious and united development of all members of the family (n. 25).

Serving Life.

The task of educating one's children is an essential part of the parents' participation in God's creative activity. "Parents are the first and foremost educators of their children" (n. 36). The parents must create a family atmosphere animated with love for God and others in order to foster a well-rounded personal and social development of the children (n. 36).

The parents' love is the basis for instilling in the children kindness, goodness, service, self-sacrifice and the other moral virtues. "Children must grow up with a correct attitude of freedom with regard to material goods by adopting a simple life style and being convinced that 'man is more precious for what he *is* than for what he *has*'" (n. 37, emphasis added).

Individualism and selfishness must be avoided by teaching the children true love and service. "The self-giving that inspires the love of husband and wife for each other [will be imitated] by the brothers and sisters" (n. 37).

Sex education, which must be controlled by the parents, must comprehend the whole person – body, emotions, and soul – so that sex is understood as a gift of self in love. Parents must also explain apostolic celibacy as the supreme form of self-giving (n. 37).

Participating in the Development of Society.

"The family is the first and vital cell of society" (n. 42). It is the first school of social life where the essential social values of truth, freedom, justice and charity are instilled. These values are essential if we are to build a civilization of love.

Each family should be conscious of its responsibility toward the community (n. 64). The family should practice hospitality by opening its home to others, especially the needy. Because the well being of the family is essential for the well being of society, society must protect the rights of the family.

Sharing in the Life and Mission of the Church.

The family plays an important role in the building up of the Kingdom of God in history (n. 49). The family should be a "domestic church" which communicates Christ's love in word and deed (n. 49). Pope Paul VI said, "[T]he family ought to be a place from which the Gospel radiates" (n. 52). It should be an evangelizer of the neighborhood of which it forms a part. John Paul similarly says, "The family has a special vocation to witness Christ by constantly radiating the joy of love and certainty of hope in the life to come" (n. 52). To bear such witness, the family must be a place of prayer. Saying the family rosary is especially recommended (n. 61).

The family also greatly contributes to the accomplishment of the Church's mission of evangelization by being the seedbed of vocations. Vocations are a crown of glory for it. A family will produce vocations if it is open to transcendent values, serves its members with joy, and accepts the daily cross of Christ in a spirit of sacrifice and self-denial (n. 53). "It is through the cross that a family attains the perfection of love" (n. 86).

The Holy Father concludes the apostolic exhortation by urging Christian families to model themselves on the Holy Family of Nazareth. He entrusts each family to Jesus, Mary and Joseph so that every Christian home may be filled with light, joy, serenity and strength (n. 86).

Redemptionis Donum
(The Gift of the Redemption).
Apostolic Exhortation dated March 25, 1984.

This apostolic exhortation addressed to members of religious orders was issued during the Holy Year of Redemption (1983-84). It is a reflection by Pope John Paul II on the vocation to the religious life in light of the mystery of the Redemption. The Holy Father expresses the Church's love for men and women religious whom he calls "a special treasure of the Church" (n. 16). He urges the members of religious orders to be faithful to their special vocation to holiness.

"Come, Follow Me."

Jesus said, "If you would be perfect, go, sell what you have and give to the poor, and you will have treasure in heaven; and come, follow me" (Mk. 10: 21, n. 3). While these words evoke the religious vocation, they also apply to the lay faithful because, as the Pope says, "[T]he call to perfection belongs to the very essence of the Christian vocation" (n. 4). Thus, all of the faithful are called to "be perfect as your heavenly Father is perfect" (Mt. 5: 48, n. 4).

By the profession of the evangelical counsels, men and women religious make a special covenant with Christ to strive towards a particular fullness of Christian life. Their vocation springs from an individual encounter with Christ's redeeming love. Just as the Lord gave himself completely in the mystery of the Redemption, he calls men and women religious to give themselves completely to the work of the Redemption as members of religious communities approved by the Church (n. 3). Their vocation has its beginning in Christ. "You did not choose me, but I chose you" (Jn. 15: 16, n. 6). Men and women religious in turn freely choose to accept the way the Lord has shown them. The self-giving love that is at the heart of the religious vocation is a special source of spiritual and supernatural energy for the Church and the world.

The "treasure in heaven" that Christ promises to those who follow in his footsteps, whether or not as members of religious orders, is not something external to the person. It is not analogous to a monetary payment for a service that one might receive on earth. Rather this treasure is found in the state of one's soul at the time of one's death. The Holy Father says that it is "not so much a 'reward' after death for the good works done following the example of the divine Teacher, but rather the eschatological fulfillment of what was hidden behind these good works here on earth, in the inner 'treasure' of the heart" (n. 5). Thus in heaven we will experience the reward of holiness in our own being — in the person we have become through our actions and correspondence to grace while on earth.

The Evangelical Counsels and Man's Redemption.

A religious is "consecrated to God in Jesus Christ as his exclusive possession" (n. 7). The religious profession creates a new bond between the person and God. It is founded, however, on the original bond that arose from the sacrament of baptism. In baptism the faithful become "dead to sin and alive to God" (Rom. 6: 11) by virtue of the grace of the Redemption. "In Christ crucified is to be found the ultimate foundation both of baptismal consecration and the profession of the evangelical counsels" (n. 7).

The evangelical counsels counteract the "lust of the flesh, the lust of the eyes and the pride of life" (1 Jn. 2: 15-17) that are part of man's inheritance from original sin. The counsels transform the human heart so that the world will "be subject to man and given to him in such a way that man himself may be perfectly given to God" (n. 9). The evangelical counsels thus aim at the renewal of both man and creation.

As indicated above, in the mystery of the Redemption are found both self-emptying through Christ's death on the cross and birth to a new life through the Resurrection. The practice of the evangelical counsels reflects this duality in that they help a person to be both less subject to sin and more responsive to grace (n. 10).

"If anyone would come after me, let him deny himself and take up his cross and follow me" (Mk. 8: 34, n. 10). By sharing in the cross, the Christian partakes of Christ's self-giving love. "The law of renunciation belongs therefore to the very essence of the Christian vocation. But it belongs in a particular way to the essence of the vocation linked to the profession of the evangelical counsels" (n. 10).

Poverty, Chastity and Obedience.

Chastity emphasizes the spousal character of a consecrated person's love of Christ. Poverty and obedience emphasize "primarily the aspect of redemptive love contained in religious consecration" (n. 11).

Choosing celibacy "for the sake of the kingdom of heaven" (Mt. 19: 12) is not only a renunciation of marriage and family life. It is also a "charismatic choice of Christ as one's exclusive Spouse" (n. 11).

The religious thus enter into a "mystical marriage with the divine Spouse in the Church" (n. 4). Celibacy is also a sign of eternal life: "a life in union with God himself through the beatific vision and the love which contains in itself and completely pervades all the other loves of the human heart" (n. 11).

"Blessed are the poor in spirit" (Mt. 5: 3, n. 12). Evangelical poverty both enriches others and testifies to the infinite richness of God (n. 12). It demonstrates that the value of the human person is in his "being," not in "having" or "possessing." "Man's real treasure is in his heart, which Christ makes one capable of 'giving' to others by the gift of self. The rich person is not the one who possesses but the one who 'gives,' the one who is capable of giving." (n. 5).

Christ became "obedient unto death, even death on a cross" (Phil. 2: 8, n. 13). In Christ's obedience is found the very essence of the Redemption. By his obedience, Christ "redeemed humanity and made it holy" (n. 13). The evangelical counsel of obedience overcomes the selfish tendency to dominate others and replaces it with the attitude of service in imitation of Christ who "came not to be served but to give his life for the ransom of many" (Mk. 10: 45, n. 13).

From the evangelical counsels comes a "total availability to the Holy Spirit" (n. 13) which has permitted men and women religious to undertake countless works of service to the Church and the world down through the ages.

In concluding the apostolic exhortation, the Holy Father invites the members of religious orders to renew their consecration according to the model of Mary, the Mother of God. "For she was called by God to the most perfect communion with his son. May she, the faithful Virgin, also be the Mother of your evangelical way" (n. 17).

Reconciliatio et Paenitentia (Reconciliation and Penance).

Post-Synodal Apostolic Exhortation dated December 2, 1984.

The theme of the 1984 Synod of Bishops was reconciliation and penance. In this post-synodal apostolic exhortation, Pope John Paul II urges the faithful to avail themselves of God's merciful love so that they may be united to God and to one another. *Reconciliation* is the re-establishment of personal relationships with God and others that have been ruptured by sin. *Penance* refers to the ascetical practices that heal the wounds of sin and permit one to live the life of Christ ever more deeply. The primary means of reconciliation in the Church is the sacrament of Penance (confession). This sacrament must be at the heart of the Church's efforts to overcome humanity's divisions. Topics covered in the document include: the meaning of reconciliation, the mystery of sin, and why mortal sins must be confessed to a priest.

The Meaning of Reconciliation.

At the beginning of his preaching Jesus tells his listeners, "Repent, and believe in the Gospel" (Mk 1: 15, n. 1). He continues to call each person to convert from sin and to live a life of grace. Sin is the radical cause of wounds and divisions among people and between people and God (n. 4).

The Holy Father uses the parable of the prodigal son (Lk. 15: 11-32) to explain the meaning of reconciliation. He says the "prodigal son is man—every human being" (n. 5). Each of us can identify with him when we yield to temptation and fall into sin. Like the prodigal son, man is tempted to separate himself from his Father God in order to lead an independent existence. He inevitably becomes disappointed, however, by the emptiness of the mirage that had fascinated him. Isolation from God in a world of his own making results in loneliness, dishonor, and exploitation. Then in the depths of his soul the sinner experiences a desire to return to communion with God. Like the father in the parable, God watches for the return of his repentant children and embraces them when they arrive. The father's loving welcome of the returning prodigal son is "a sign of the mercy of God who is always willing to forgive" (n. 5). The parable teaches us that "reconciliation is principally a gift of the heavenly Father" (n. 5).

Through his passion and death, Jesus Christ made reconciliation possible in its twofold aspect of liberation from sin and communion with God. Christ entrusted the Church with the ministry of bringing salvation to the whole world in his name. "To evoke conversion and penance in man's heart and to offer him the gift of reconciliation is the specific mission of the Church as she continues the redemptive work of her divine Founder" (n. 23).

The Mystery of Sin.

Sin is an offense against God. It is an act by which a creature knowingly and freely opposes the will of God, violating the law of good and freely submitting to the yoke of evil.

The Holy Father explains how sin harms the sinner. "As a personal act, sin has its first and most important consequences in the sinner himself: in his relationship with God, who is the very foundation of human life; and also in his spirit, weakening his will and clouding his intellect" (n. 16).

Each individual's sin, however, in some way affects others. "A soul that lowers itself through sin drags down the Church and in some way the whole world. There is no sin, not even the most intimate and secret one, the most strictly individual one, that exclusively concerns the person committing it" (n. 16).

The impact of sin on the family was apparent in the Garden of Eden where the first sin ended with man and woman pointing an accusing finger at each other. Later we see a brother hating his brother and taking his life.

The consequences of sin for society are shown in the story of Babel. We see that man's rupture with God leads to the shattering of the human family. The people of Babel found themselves divided in speech, divided among themselves and incapable of agreement. The lesson of Babel is that man can try to build a world without God, but such a world will turn against him. "In the story of Babel the exclusion of God is presented not so much under the aspect of opposition to him as of forgetfulness and indifference towards him, as if God were of no relevance in the sphere of man's projects" (n. 14). It is not hard to draw parallels between Babel and modern society.

John Paul affirms the distinction between mortal sin, which causes a complete loss of grace, and venial sin, which does not. If unforgiven, mortal sin leads to eternal punishment (n. 17). Recourse to sacramental confession is necessary when only one mortal sin has been committed (n. 27).

Man will not have a "sense of sin" unless his moral conscience is linked to a sense of God. "When the conscience is weakened the sense of God is also obscured, and as a result, with the loss of this decisive inner point of reference, the sense of sin is lost" (n. 18). The sense of sin has been undermined by "secularism" which "advocates a humanism totally without God, completely centered upon the cult of action and production and caught in the heady enthusiasm of consumerism and pleasure seeking, unconcerned with the danger of 'losing one's soul'" (n. 18).

"The restoration of a sense of sin is the first way of facing the grave spiritual crisis looming over man today. But the sense of sin will be restored only through a clear reminder of the unchangeable principles of reason and faith which the Church has always upheld" (n. 18).

While man is dragged down by the mystery of sin (*"mysterium iniquitatis"*), he is also lifted up by the mystery of God's merciful love (*"mysterium pietatis"*). God's infinite, loving kindness should be recognized as a vital, active principle that evokes in a soul a movement of conversion that sets it on a path toward reconciliation and redemption (n. 20). Divine mercy "is a love more powerful than sin, stronger than death" (n. 22). Man must cooperate with grace, however, by making a personal effort in the struggle against sin.

The Church facilitates penance and reconciliation primarily through catechesis and the sacraments. Catechesis includes spreading the truth about divine mercy and the need for repentance and personal conversion. The Church must never fail to teach the truth about death, judgment, heaven and hell (n. 26).

The Sacrament of Penance.

While each sacrament is in its own way a sign of reconciliation, the sacrament of Penance is the most efficacious means of reconciliation. It is the primary way of obtaining forgiveness and remission of sins committed after Baptism. This sacrament "gives to every Christian and the whole community of believers the certainty of forgiveness through the power of the redeeming blood of Christ" (n. 28). Because the sacrament of Penance is so often neglected today, it is necessary to frequently affirm its critical role in the Church's salvific mission. The Risen Christ told the Apostles, "Whose sins you shall forgive, they are forgiven. Whose sins you shall retain, they are retained" (Jn. 20: 23). The Pope describes this ability as "one of the most awe inspiring innovations in the Gospel" (n. 28). As heirs of the Apostles, priests have the power to forgive sins in Christ's name.

Making a good confession requires an *examination of conscience* in which one admits the sins he has committed, having *contrition* (or sorrow) for his sins including a resolution not to sin again, *confession* of one's sins to a priest, receiving *absolution* which is the efficacious sign of God's forgiveness, and performing the *penance* (or "satisfaction") given by the priest as a sign of one's personal commitment to begin a new life. The penitent should also give thanks to God for the forgiveness he has received.

The Holy Father explains why a Catholic must confess his sins to a priest rather than only seek forgiveness directly from God. The first reason is that doing so is the will of Christ. "It would be foolish, as well as presumptuous, to wish arbitrarily to disregard the means of grace and salvation which the Lord has provided and to claim to receive forgiveness while doing without the sacrament which was instituted by Christ precisely for forgiveness" (n. 31).

Secondly, confession is demanded by the nature of the sacrament of Penance. The sacrament involves a kind of judicial action that takes place before a tribunal. It also has a medicinal character since it heals the wounds caused by sin. "Whether as a tribunal of mercy or a place of spiritual healing, under both aspects the sacrament requires a knowledge of the sinner's heart in order to be able to judge and absolve, to cure and heal. Precisely for this reason, the sacrament involves on the part of the penitent a sincere and complete confession of sins" (n. 31).

Thirdly, the sacrament of Penance reconciles the penitent with the Church which was injured by his sins. The priest represents the ecclesial community as it welcomes anew the forgiven sinner (n. 31).

Finally, confession of sins to a priest serves as an exercise in humility and mortification that will strengthen the sinner and help him to persevere in his resolution not to sin again.

The Pope concludes the document with an expression of hope that, through recourse to divine mercy, the faithful will experience the love and unity to which they are called.

Christifideles Laici
(On the Vocation and Mission of the Lay Faithful).
Post-Synodal Apostolic Exhortation dated December 30, 1988.

Christifideles Laici was issued by Pope John Paul II after the 1987 Synod of Bishops on the laity. The purpose of this post-synodal apostolic exhortation is to promote a deeper awareness among the laity of their responsibilities – both individually and collectively – in carrying out the Church's mission. In a word, the *vocation* of the laity is personal sanctity; the special *mission* of the laity is the sanctification of the world.

The Pope begins the document by saying that the state of affairs in society today "calls with a particular urgency for the action of the lay faithful...It is not permissible for anyone to remain idle" (n. 3). "The lay faithful," he continues, "have an essential and irreplaceable role [in the Church's mission]. Through them, the Church of Christ is made present in the world as a sign and source of hope and love" (n. 7).

The Dignity of the Lay Faithful.

The Holy Father refers throughout the document to the parable of the vineyard (Mt. 20, 1-16). The laity are the laborers who must transform the world (symbolized by the vineyard) according to the plan of God (n. 3).

Lay people are not meant to be second-class citizens in the Church. John Paul proclaims a radical "equality among all the baptized in Christ" (n. 15). Vatican II stated that all members of the Church "have the same filial grace and the same vocation to perfection" (n. 15). The laity, like ordained ministers and members of religious orders, "are in their own way made sharers in the priestly, prophetic and kingly offices of Christ" (n. 9).

The chart below indicates in matrix fashion how ordained ministers, religious, and lay people share in the offices (or "missions") of Christ. The three groups are presented side-by-side to reflect their equality. Needless to say, the mission of each group is a very difficult one. Vatican II and the Holy Father reject a vision of the Church that portrays ordained ministers and religious at the top of the organization chart with the laity at the bottom as if the former were the officers and the latter were only the troops.

How do lay people participate in the three missions of Christ? They participate in the *priestly mission* by offering to God – in union with the sacrifice of the Mass – their daily activities which they strive to carry out with perfection. Vatican II says, "For [the laity], work, prayers and apostolic endeavors, their ordinary married and family life…their mental and physical relaxation…even the hardships of life if patiently borne—all of these become spiritual sacrifices acceptable to God through Jesus Christ. During the celebration of the Eucharist these sacrifices are most lovingly offered to the Father" (n. 13). (Do I make such an offering of my daily duties to God when I attend Holy Mass?)

The lay faithful participate in the *prophetic (or "teaching") mission* by proclaiming the Gospel in word and deed. To carry out this mission, one should strive to acquire a solid doctrinal formation, for example, by studying the *Catechism of the Catholic Church.* (Do I spread Catholic doctrine, for example, by talking about God and moral issues with my friends at the appropriate times?)

The lay faithful participate in the *kingly (or "ruling") mission* by spreading Christ's kingdom in history. "In ordering creation to the authentic well-being of humanity...[the laity] share in the exercise of power with which the Risen Christ draws all things to himself..." (n. 13). The laity are thus called to shape society with a Christian spirit by combining their professional skills with a Christian conscience. (Do I apply a Christian conscience in carrying out my professional work?)

The laity are distinguished by their "secular" character. The "world" is the place where they fulfill their Christian vocation. They are in the world because that is where God called them to be. As stated by Vatican II, "Led by the spirit of the Gospel, [the laity] contribute to the sanctification of the world from within, as a leaven, by fulfilling their particular duties" (n. 15). The Pope says, "The world itself is destined to glorify God the Father in Christ" (n. 15). It is the laity's task to insure that all aspects of society —law, business, entertainment, medicine, education, etc.—in fact give glory to God. (Does my professional environment give glory to God?)

The world should be seen as the "secular dimension" of the Church. "Thus, for the lay faithful to be present and active in the world is not only an anthropological and sociological reality, but in a specific way, a theological and ecclesiological reality as well" (n. 15). The secular character of the laity in the theological sense refers to their vocation to participate in the work of creation through the fulfillment of their professional and other secular duties. Thus, performing one's professional work has theological meaning. As stated by St. Paul, "Whatever you do in word or in deed, do everything in the name of the Lord Jesus" (Col. 3: 17).

John Paul commends those lay people who are striving to live their faith to the full in the middle of the world: "The eyes of faith behold a wonderful scene: that of a countless number of lay people, both men and women, busy at work in their daily life and activity, oftentimes far from view and quite unacclaimed by the world, unknown to the world's great personages but nevertheless looked upon in love by the Father, untiring laborers who work in the Lord's vineyard. Confident and steadfast through the power of God's grace, these are the humble yet great builders of the Kingdom of God in history" (n. 17). (Do I aspire to be like these men and women?)

The laity cannot fulfill their mission without personal holiness. The Holy Father reiterates that "the faithfulness and growth of the branches depends on their remaining united to the vine" (n. 17).

The Participation of the Lay Faithful in the Life of the Church.

Fulfilling one's Christian mission requires joining with other members of the Church. For example, it is good to be active in one's parish which "brings the Church into the neighborhood" (n. 27). "A member of the lay faithful can never remain in isolation from the community, but must live in a continual interaction with others, with a lively sense of fellowship" (n. 20).

Each individual contributes to the good of the Church and simultaneously shares in the common riches of the Church (n. 28). Each member of the lay faithful has been "entrusted with a unique task which

Apostolic Exhortations   103

cannot be done by another and which is fulfilled for the good of all" (n. 28).

The Responsibility of the Lay Faithful in the Church's Mission.

The Pope returns to the biblical image of the vine and the branches by reminding the faithful that branches are expected to bear fruit. "He who abides in me and I in him, he it is that bears much fruit" (Jn. 15, 5). "The hour has come for a re-evangelization" (n. 34). "This is a great adventure, both challenging and wonderful" (n. 64). We will bear apostolic fruit only if we are consistent Christians who are united to Christ in grace.

A key part of re-evangelization is promoting the dignity of the person. The dignity of each person rests on his being an image of God destined for eternal life. "The value of one person transcends all the material world" (n. 37). Thus, persons must be valued for what they *are*, not for what they *have*. We have to stand up for human rights, especially the right to life.

Respect for the dignity of the person demands recognition of the religious dimension of the individual. This has to enter into all political, social, and economic considerations. Christians must participate actively in public life which must be concerned with the pursuit of the common good (n. 42).

We must evangelize popular culture which is becoming disassociated not only from the Christian faith but also from human values. The lay faithful must be present in the places where culture is formed such as institutions of higher learning, scientific research, and artistic and literary creativity. Such a presence will permit the purification and elevation of culture through the influence of the Gospel message (n. 44). As stated by Vatican II, "The good news of Christ continually renews the life and culture of fallen humanity. It combats and removes the error and evil which flow from the attraction of sin" (n. 44).

Professionals in the mass media in particular must be animated by a passion for truth, a respect for the dignity of individuals, and a desire to elevate the authentic culture of society (n. 44).

Laborers in the Lord's Vineyard.

During all stages of life (childhood, youth, adulthood and old age), in all states of life (marriage, celibacy or widowhood), in all states of health or sickness, and in all professional and social circumstances, lay men and women are called to participate in the life and mission of the Church (n. 56).

There are an infinite number of ways for them to work in the vineyard of the Lord, building up the Mystical Body of Christ. The Holy Father reiterates that, just as each person has a unique life story, so each member of the Church "is called by name to make a special contribution to the coming of the Kingdom of God" (n. 56).

The Formation of the Lay Faithful.

To achieve the unique mission that God has entrusted to each of us, we need formation. Similarly, it is not enough just to want to be a doctor. A person must study medicine and undergo years of training. To fulfill our Christian vocation we also need certain "skills."

"The fundamental objective of the formation of the lay faithful is an ever clearer discovery of one's vocation and the ever greater willingness to live it" (n. 58). The main categories of formation are spiritual, human, and doctrinal. Through *spiritual formation,* we grow in interior life and friendship with our Lord. This is fostered primarily by prayer, receiving the sacraments, and reading the Gospel. Through *human formation,* we grow in virtue, character and personal maturity. Through *doctrinal formation,* we grow in knowledge of the Catholic faith and the principles of morality. We need to grow in each of these areas of formation throughout our lives.

Our formation is aimed at giving us "unity of life" so that there will not be a split between our spiritual life and our secular life. Sometimes it is difficult for us to accept changes in our life that are necessary to fulfill God's will. The Pope encourages us by saying, "Only the branch which does not fear being pruned by the heavenly vine dresser can bear much fruit" (n. 63).

The Holy Father closes the document with a prayer to the Blessed Virgin in which he asks her to enable each of us to do our part in establishing on earth the civilization of truth and love that God wills.

The Salvific Mission of Jesus Christ
the One Savior of the World
As Achieved Through the Church

	DUTIES OF ORDAINED MINISTERS	DUTIES OF RELIGIOUS	DUTIES OF THE LAITY	GIFT
PROPHETIC OFFICE OF CHRIST	Preaching the Gospel	Testimony of the Evangelical Counsels	Witness of the Christian Life in Word and Deed	Truth
PRIESTLY OFFICE OF CHRIST	Ministering the Sacraments	Special Consecration to Christ	Offering One's Daily Activities to God through the Mass	Grace
KINGLY OFFICE OF CHRIST	Pastoral Guidance of the Church	Charitable Services	Ordering all Secular Realities to God's Plan	Christian Life in Community

Redemptoris Custos
(Guardian of the Redeemer).
Apostolic Exhortation dated August 15, 1989.

Redemptoris Custos is a reflection on St. Joseph, the person whom Pope Leo XIII described as "the lawful and natural guardian, head and defender of the Holy Family" (n. 28). In this apostolic exhortation, Pope John Paul II urges the faithful to grow in prayerful devotion to St. Joseph, to trust in his fatherly care and to imitate his noble example of dedicated service to the Lord. The Pope begins the document by reminding the faithful that, "just as St. Joseph took loving care of Mary and gladly dedicated himself to Jesus Christ's upbringing, he likewise watches over and protects Christ's Mystical Body, that is, the Church" (n. 1).

St. Joseph is a role model for all Christians, but especially for husbands and fathers. John Paul explains why St. Joseph is an ideal model of obedience to God's will, dedicated fatherhood, the sanctification of work and ordinary life, and interior life.

Devotion to St. Joseph.

Our Lord's guardian passed largely unnoticed in Western Christianity for some 15 centuries. Then in the 1500's, the Spanish mystic, St. Theresa of Avila, promoted the renewal of veneration to St. Joseph (n. 25). She was moved by Joseph's silence —none of his words are contained in scripture — and the aura of deep contemplation that he combined with the fulfillment of his duties.

In 1870, during a period of great turmoil for the Church, Pope Bl. Pius IX declared St. Joseph to be the Patron of the Universal Church. The Pope sought protection from the person "into whose custody God entrusted his most precious treasurers" (n. 1). In 1889, when the Church was again under serious attack in many places, Pope Leo XIII issued a major encyclical, *Quamquam Pluries*, on devotion to St. Joseph. He appealed to St. Joseph's fatherly love with the prayer: "Just as you once saved the Child Jesus from mortal danger, so now defend God's holy Church from the snares of her enemies and from all adversity" (n. 31). The present document was issued on the hundredth anniversary of the publication of Leo's encyclical.

In 1955 Pope Pius XII instituted the feast day of St. Joseph the Worker which is celebrated on May 1 (n. 22). He intended to provide a Christian alternative to the socialist "May Day" celebrations that took place on that day. This feast day is an opportunity to recall the Christian meaning of all honest work, especially manual labor. John Paul comments, "At the workbench where he plied his trade with Jesus, Joseph brought human work closer to the mystery of the Redemption" (n. 22).

In 1962, at the close of the first session of Vatican II, Pope Bl. John XXIII added St. Joseph's name to the Roman Canon of the Mass (the present Eucharistic Prayer I) after the name of Mary and before the names of the apostles, popes and martyrs (n. 6).

Obedience of Faith.

St. Joseph is a model of obedience because he most faithfully carried out God's commands (n. 30). He responded positively to the will of God when it was communicated to him (n. 4). Like Mary, Joseph's life was a pilgrimage of faith, and he remained faithful until the end (n. 17). "Obedience of faith" is the full submission of mind and will to God as he reveals himself (n. 4).

Joseph's most dramatic moment of obedience came when he was told by an angel to rise in the middle of the night and flee with Jesus and Mary to Egypt (Mt. 2: 13, n. 14). Tradition tells us that the Holy Family departed Bethlehem just before the arrival of Herod's soldiers who proceeded to massacre the innocents. If Joseph hadn't obeyed immediately, the life of Jesus would have been lost. From this we learn that the extent of a father's obedience to God's commands has a great impact on the well being of his family.

A Model Husband and Father.

The juridical basis of Joseph's fatherhood was his marriage to Mary (n. 9). St. Augustine said, "By reason of their faithful marriage both [Mary and Joseph] deserve to be called Christ's parents, not only his mother, but also his father, who was a parent in the same way that he was his mother's spouse: in mind, not in the flesh" (n. 7).

Mary and Joseph were united by a bond of virginal and marital love. These two kinds of love represent the mystery of the Church which is both virgin and spouse. Thus, the marriage of Mary and Joseph symbolizes the Church (n. 20). The Pope repeats what he said in *Familiaris Consortio*, "Marriage and virginity are two ways of expressing and living the one mystery of the Covenant of God with his people" (n. 20).

Joseph fulfilled all of his fatherly duties. He was the overseer of the Lord's birth and gave him the name "Jesus" (Lk. 2: 22, n. 12). He had the task of "raising" Jesus, that is, feeding, clothing, and educating him in the Law and in a trade (n. 16). He also carried out the significant task of officially inserting the name "Jesus, son of Joseph of Nazareth" (cf., Jn. 1: 45) in the Registry of the Roman Empire. The Holy Father says, "This registration clearly shows that Jesus belonged to the human race as a man among men, a citizen of the world subject to laws and civil institutions, but also 'savior of the world'" (n. 9).

The Holy Family is the prototype and example for all Christian families. The mission of the family is above all to guard, reveal and communicate love. Such love is a living reflection of and a real sharing in God's love for humanity (n. 7). Like many families, the Holy Family experienced hardship: first the poverty in Bethlehem, then the exile in Egypt (n. 21).

"St. Joseph was called by God to serve the mission of Jesus directly through the exercise of his fatherhood" (n. 8). As stated by Pope Paul VI, Joseph's fatherhood was expressed concretely "in his having made his life a service, a sacrifice to the mystery of the Incarnation and to the redemptive mission connected with it … [He made] a total gift of self, of his life and work … [He] turned his human vocation to domestic love into a superhuman oblation of self … at the service of the Messiah growing up in his house" (n. 8).

Similarly, married men are called to serve the mission of Jesus through their fatherhood. The sanctification of the family, "that sanctuary of love and cradle of life" (n. 7), is of fundamental importance in the plan of salvation. If the spouses are faithful to their Christian vocation, this will enrich their marriage. Love of God molds human love to perfection. If a husband and wife love God, their love for each other will be transformed into an authentic communion according to the model of the Blessed Trinity (n. 19). On the other hand, if a person lacks love of God and seeks from his or her spouse the happiness that can only come from God, he or she will be frustrated and disappointed.

Sanctification of Work and Ordinary Life.

"Work was the daily expression of love in the life of the family of Nazareth" (n. 22). Joseph was a carpenter, and Jesus was known as the carpenter's son. Joseph teaches us that work is a human good and that industriousness is an important human virtue.

In Joseph we see the critical importance of the sanctification of ordinary life. Pope Paul VI said, "St. Joseph is proof that in order to be a good and genuine follower of Christ, there is no need of great things: it is enough to have common, simple and human virtues, but they must be true and authentic" (n. 22). The two greatest saints, Mary and Joseph, were not much in the eyes of the world. Similarly, ordinary lay people will be effective in transforming the world if they are steadfast in their efforts to sanctify themselves, their work and their communities.

Model of Interior Life.

"The total sacrifice, whereby Joseph surrendered his whole existence to the demands of the Messiah's coming into his home, becomes understandable only in the light of his profound interior life" (n. 26). From this Joseph received the strength to fulfill the demands made on him. His contemplative spirit permitted him to see them as demands of love (n. 27). Similarly, we must have interior life if we are to be faithful to the mission entrusted to us. Interior life is founded on prayer, the Gospel and the sacraments. We must "make time" for these devotions each day if we are to persevere in fulfilling our family and other responsibilities.

The Pope ends the apostolic exhortation by urging the faithful to follow St. Joseph's example and to invoke his patronage as they commit themselves to the evangelization of the world (n. 29).

Pastores Dabo Vobis
(I Will Give You Shepherds).
Post-Synodal Apostolic Exhortation dated March 25, 1992.

This post-synodal apostolic exhortation on "the formation of priests in the circumstances of the present day" followed the 1990 Synod of Bishops on this subject. The document takes its title from the words of the Lord to the prophet Jeremiah, "I will give you shepherds after my own heart" (Jer. 3: 15, n. 1). The role of the priest is "to proclaim the Gospel to the world and to build up the Church in the name and person of Christ the head and shepherd" (n. 15).

In the face of the current "crisis of priestly vocations" (n. 1), the Holy Father convened the Synod to reflect on the life and ministry of priests and the formation they require in today's world. He considers the formation of priests to be "one of the most demanding and important tasks for the future of the evangelization of humanity" (n. 2).

The Nature and Mission of the Ministerial Priesthood.

"Every high priest chosen from among men is appointed to act on behalf of men in relation to God" (Heb. 5: 1, n. 5). The priest finds his identity in Christ, "the one high priest of the new and eternal covenant" (n. 12). By virtue of the consecration he receives in the sacrament of Holy Orders, the priest is sent forth "to live and work by the power of the Holy Spirit in the service of the Church for the salvation of the world" (n. 12). As indicated by our Lord's words, "As the Father has sent me, so I send you" (Jn. 20: 21, n. 14), priests are empowered to continue Christ's ministry of reconciliation, of shepherding the flock of God and of teaching. A priest embodies Christ's way of life and makes him visible to the flock entrusted to his care (n. 15).

The ministerial priesthood and the common priesthood of the faithful differ essentially and not only in degree. They are, however, ordered to one another since they are both derived from the one priesthood of Christ (n. 17). Priests have the task of helping the laity to exercise faithfully and fully their common priesthood. "[T]he ministerial priesthood does not of itself signify a greater degree of holiness with regard to the common priesthood of the faithful" (n. 17).

Speaking as a priest, the Holy Father states, "Our priestly life and activity continue the life and activity of Christ himself. Here lies our identity, our true dignity, the source of our joy, the very basis of our life" (n. 18).

The Spiritual Life of the Priest.

The sacrament of Holy Orders is a source of holiness and a call to sanctification. "Holiness is intimacy with God; it is the imitation of Christ who was poor, chaste and humble; it is unreserved love for souls and a giving of oneself on their behalf and for their true good; it is love for the Church which is holy and wants to be holy" (n. 33). While all Christians "must be perfect as your heavenly Father is perfect" (Mt. 5: 48), priests are especially bound to strive for perfection because they are consecrated to God in a new way by their ordination. They have become living instruments of Christ (n. 21).

The spiritual life of priests should be marked by a fundamental attitude of service to the People of God. Because priests are configured to Jesus the good shepherd, they are called to image his pastoral charity. "Pastoral charity is the virtue by which we imitate Christ in his self-giving and service" (n. 23). Priests are also called to image Jesus as the spouse of the Church. They witness Christ's spousal love when they love people with a generous and pure heart (n. 22).

Personal holiness is necessary for the fruitful fulfillment of the priestly ministry. The priest's call to lead the ecclesiastical community demands an intense spiritual life (n. 26). In order to be an effective minister of the word of God, a priest must develop a great personal familiarity with sacred scripture through study and meditation. As the minister of the sacraments and celebrant of the Liturgy, a priest must live a deep unity between the exercise of his ministry and his spiritual life. In particular, a priest must avail himself of the sacrament of Penance so as to become a witness of God's mercy towards sinners.

Because priests are called to a radical living of the Gospel, they should practice the evangelical counsels of obedience, chastity and poverty. Priests must live the evangelical counsel of obedience because, like Christ, they must be ready to do, not their own will, but the will of him who sent them (cf., Jn. 4: 34, n. 28). The priest serves the Church within her hierarchical structure and must obey her ecclesiastical laws and authorities. A priest must especially obey his diocesan bishop or ordinary.

Priests live the evangelical counsel of chastity though celibacy. Celibacy permits a priest to more easily devote himself to God with an undivided heart (cf., 1 Cor. 7: 32-34). As stated by Vatican II, "This perfect continence for love of the kingdom of heaven has always been held in high esteem by the Church as a sign and stimulus of love, and as a singular source of spiritual fertility in the world" (n. 29). Celibacy is a positive enrichment of the priesthood and a precious gift of God to his Church. It is also a visible sign of the world to come. The Church requires celibacy of its priests because the "Church, as the Spouse of Jesus Christ, wishes to be loved by the priest in the total and exclusive manner in which Jesus Christ her head and spouse loved her. Priestly celibacy, then, is the gift of self in and with Christ to his Church and expresses the priest's service to the Church in and with the Lord" (n. 29).

Priests live the evangelical counsel of poverty by having a simple and austere lifestyle, having learned the generous renunciation of superfluous things. In this way they follow the example of Christ who, though he was rich, became poor for love of us (cf., 2 Cor. 8: 9, n. 30).

The spiritual life of a priest should also be "profoundly marked by a missionary zeal and dynamism" (n. 32). Priests have the duty to form the community entrusted to them as a truly missionary community.

Promoting Vocations to the Priesthood.

Every priestly vocation is the result of the love of God who calls and the freedom of the individual who responds lovingly to him (n. 36). These two aspects of vocation, God's gratuitous gift and the responsible freedom of human beings, are expressed in the calling of the twelve apostles by Jesus who "went up into the hills, and called to him those whom he desired, and they came to him" (Mk. 3: 13, n. 36).

The present crisis of priestly vocations is rooted in a general crisis of faith (n. 37). The Church's effort to promote vocations must be built on faith and sustained by it. As stated by Vatican II, "The duty of fostering vocations falls on the whole Christian community, and they should discharge it principally by living full Christian lives" (n. 41).

A special responsibility falls on the Christian family which must provide favorable conditions for the birth of vocations. To be disposed to receiving a vocation, boys and young men must be taught to have a life of piety and learn the value of sacrifice and self-giving. Promoting vocations also includes "direct preaching on the mystery of vocation in the Church [and] on the value of the ministerial priesthood" (n. 39).

The Formation of Candidates for the Priesthood.

Candidates for the priesthood must receive human, spiritual, intellectual and pastoral formation. Human formation, a person's growth in character, is the foundation of all other formation. Future priests should cultivate human qualities such as love for the truth, loyalty, respect for every person, a sense of justice, compassion, integrity, and especially being balanced in judgment and behavior (n. 43). Of special importance is the capacity to relate to others. "This demands that the priest not be arrogant, or quarrelsome, but affable, hospitable, sincere in his words and heart, prudent and discreet, generous and ready to serve, capable of opening himself to clear and brotherly relationships and of encouraging the same in others, and quick to understand, forgive and console" (n. 43).

Affective maturity, which is the result of an education in true and responsible love, is a decisive factor in the formation of candidates for the priesthood. "Affective maturity presupposes an awareness that love has a central role in human life" (n. 44). One's education regarding sexuality should present chastity as a virtue that develops a person's authentic maturity and makes him capable of respecting and fostering the "nuptial meaning of the body," that is, the human body's capacity to express love as a gift of self (n. 44). "Thus the candidate, who is called to celibacy, will find in affective maturity a firm support to live chastity in faithfulness and joy" (n. 44).

The aim of spiritual formation is to enable the candidates "to live in intimate and unceasing union with God" (n. 45). They should seek Christ in prayer, Holy Scripture, the sacraments of Holy Eucharist and Penance, the Divine Office and in other people, especially children, the poor, the sick, sinners and unbelievers. They should especially love and reverence the Virgin Mary (n. 45).

The goal of intellectual formation is "an ever deeper knowledge of the divine mysteries" (n. 51). This requires the study of philosophy which is a guarantee of the "certainty of truth" — the only firm basis for a total giving of oneself to Jesus and to the Church. The Holy Father asks, "If we are not certain about the truth, how can we put our whole life on the line, how can we have the strength to challenge others' way of living?" (n. 52).

The intellectual formation of the future priest is based above all on the study of theology. Theological formation will lead the candidate to a "unified vision of the truths which God revealed in Jesus Christ and of the Church's experience of faith" (n. 54). It should include the study of the Church's social doctrine which is an essential component of the new evangelization.

The object of the pastoral formation of the candidates is "to make them shepherds of souls after the example of our Lord Jesus Christ, teacher, priest and shepherd" (n. 57). Candidates should be trained to undertake the ministry of the shepherd so that they can win souls for Christ by becoming the servant of all.

Apostolic Exhortations   119

The seminary should be, not only a place to live and study, but also a true Christian community built on deep friendship and charity. The model for the seminary is the group of twelve apostles gathered around Jesus listening to his word (cf., Mk. 3: 14). The bishops should feel a grave responsibility in selecting professors and other seminary personnel. They should be people of faith who love the Church and who are totally faithful to its Magisterium (n. 67).

The Ongoing Formation of Priests.

Just as St. Paul exhorted Timothy "to rekindle the gift of God that is within you" (2 Tim. 1: 6, n. 70), a priest must continually seek personal growth and renewal. "Every life is a constant path towards maturity, a maturity which cannot be obtained except by constant formation" (n. 70). A priest must strive to grow in the human virtues in order to be able to better understand and respond to the needs of others. His spiritual life must grow in a personal, free and conscious way through an ever greater conformity to Christ. His intellectual life must be fostered through continual theological and cultural study. He must grow in pastoral charity so that he can become an ever clearer image of Jesus the good shepherd. Without continuing formation, the priest risks succumbing to activism which would prevent him from being an effective steward of the mysteries of God. Priests who keep alive their desire to learn and grow will enjoy a youthfulness of spirit (n. 79).

The ongoing formation of priests should also result in ever greater communion among priests and with the bishop. The presbyterate should be a true family, a fraternity arising not from ties of flesh and blood but from the grace of Holy Orders. The loneliness that a priest can sometimes experience is overcome by regular contact with the bishop, mutual cooperation and friendship among priests and good relations with the lay faithful (n. 74).

The Pope concludes the apostolic exhortation by urging the entire People of God to pray and work tirelessly for priestly vocations. He especially appeals to families, and mothers in particular, to be generous in giving their sons to the Lord when he calls them to the priesthood. The words of Elizabeth to Mary apply in a sense to such mothers of priests, "Blessed are you among women, and blessed is the fruit of your womb!" (Lk. 1: 42, n. 82).

The Holy Father ends with a prayer to Mary, Mother of Jesus Christ and Mother of Priests, to protect and accompany all those who have been called to the priestly ministry.

Vita Consecrata
(The Consecrated Life).
Post-Synodal Apostolic Exhortation dated March 25, 1996.

The topic of the 1994 Synod of Bishops was the consecrated life and its mission in the Church and the world. Following the synods on the laity and the priesthood, this synod completed the treatment of the distinctive "states of life" in the Catholic Church. In this post-synodal apostolic exhortation, Pope John Paul II explains the nature of the vocation to the consecrated life and the special mission entrusted to consecrated persons. The Holy Father thanks God for the priceless gift of the consecrated life that continues to contribute in a profound way to the renewal of the world.

The Nature of the Vocation to the Consecrated Life.

Consecrated persons dedicate themselves completely to God by making a special consecration to him through the profession of the evangelical counsels of poverty, chastity and obedience (n. 15). "By professing the evangelical counsels, consecrated persons not only make Christ the whole meaning of their lives, but strive to produce in themselves as far as possible 'that form of life that he, as the Son of God, accepted in entering the world'" (n. 16).

Consecrated life is an expression of a "radical gift of self for love of the Lord Jesus and, in him, of every member of the human family" (n. 3). Just as Jesus called some of his disciples to leave all things and follow him, consecrated persons are called to put their lives at his service, leaving everything behind (n. 14).

They imitate not only Jesus but also Mary "who willingly put herself at the service of God's plan by the total gift of self" (n. 18).

The consecrated life is made possible by a special vocation from God (cf., Jn. 15: 16). It is above all a call to personal holiness "which consists in the perfection of love" (n. 30). It is a great honor for a family if one of its members is blessed with such a vocation (n. 107).

The deepest meaning of the evangelical counsels is revealed when they are seen in relation to the Holy Trinity. Chastity, as a manifestation of an undivided heart (cf., 1 Cor. 7: 32-34), is a reflection of the infinite love that exists among the three divine Persons. Poverty, which proclaims that God is man's only real treasure, is lived according to the example of Christ who, "though he was rich ... became poor" (2 Cor. 8: 9). It is an expression of the total gift of self which the three divine Persons make to each other. Obedience, practiced in imitation of Christ whose food was to do the Father's will (cf., Jn. 4: 34), is a reflection of the loving harmony among the three divine Persons (n. 21).

Growing in Personal Holiness.

A consecrated person is usually a member of a religious order, a society of apostolic life or a secular institute (n. 2). "When the Church approves a form of consecrated life or an institute, she confirms that in its spiritual and apostolic charism are found all of the objective requisites for achieving personal and communal perfection according to the Gospel" (n. 93). A consecrated person, therefore, needs to be faithful to the founding charism and spiritual heritage of his or her institute (n. 36).

"[T]he consecrated life should be nourished from the wellspring of a sound and deep spirituality" (n. 93). The spiritual life of a consecrated person is developed through such practices as eucharistic adoration, receiving the sacraments, praying the Divine Office and performing the ascetic practices of his or her institute (n. 38). A filial relationship to Mary is also a most effective help for advancing in one's vocation and living it fully (n. 28).

After joining an order or institute, a person receives human, cultural, spiritual, and pastoral formation to enable him or her to develop into a mature member (n. 65). In the work of formation "special importance must be given to the interior freedom of consecrated persons, their affective maturity, their ability to communicate with others, especially in their own community, their serenity of spirit, their compassion for those who are suffering, their love for the truth and a correspondence between their actions and their words" (n. 71). The need to receive formation never ends. "Continuing formation, whether in institutes of apostolic or contemplative life, is an intrinsic requirement of religious consecration" (n. 69).

In most cases consecrated persons live in a religious community such as a monastery, convent or religious house. The members of such communities strive to live united in Christ with "one heart and one soul" (Acts. 4: 32, n. 21). "Such fraternal life, understood as a shared life in love, is an eloquent sign of ecclesial communion" (n. 42). By practicing evangelical discipleship, consecrated persons commit themselves to fulfilling the Lord's "new commandment" to love one another as he has loved us (cf., Jn. 13: 34, n. 42). In religious communities solitude is overcome through concern for one another, and wounds are healed through forgiveness (n. 45).

The cross is ever present in the life of a consecrated person. "It is in the contemplation of the crucified Christ that all vocations find their inspiration" (n. 23). The beauty and power of God's love is fully revealed by Christ on the cross (n. 24). The fidelity of consecrated persons to God is confirmed by their acceptance of sufferings for the sake of completing in their own flesh "what is lacking in Christ's afflictions" (Col. 1: 24, n. 24). The complete self-offering of a consecrated person was rightly described by St. Thomas Aquinas as a "genuine holocaust" (n. 17).

The life of a consecrated person thus should be one of unceasing conversion, progressive conformity to Christ, and ever increasing service to others (n. 36).

The Mission of the Consecrated Life.

"[T]he sense of mission is at the very heart of every form of consecrated life" (n. 25). The primary mission of the consecrated life is to manifest God's love in the world. This is accomplished first of all through the personal witness of a truly Christian life. "The more consecrated persons allow themselves to be conformed to Christ, the more Christ is made present and active in the world for the salvation of all" (n. 72).

Wearing a distinctive habit or emblem, consecrated persons are "eschatological witnesses," that is, they are signs of the everlasting life that lies beyond the grave. They are reminders to all that "here we have no lasting city" (Heb. 13: 14) because our ultimate home is heaven (n. 26).

Members of contemplative orders are "in a special way an image of Christ praying on the mountain" (n. 32). "Monasticism and contemplative life are a constant reminder that the primacy of God gives full meaning and joy to human lives, because men and women are made for God, and their hearts are restless until they rest in him" (n. 27).

Consecrated persons who are engaged in the active life (such as missionary work, teaching, nursing, and caring for the homeless) manifest Christ "in his proclamation of the kingdom of God to the multitudes, in his healing of the sick and the suffering, [and] in his work of converting sinners to a better life" (n. 32).

Christ's washing of the feet of the apostles at the Last Supper reveals the depth of God's love for humanity. It also indicates that the meaning of the Christian life is found in a life of self-giving love, of practical and generous service. Just as the Son of Man "came not to be served but to serve" (Mt. 20: 28), the consecrated life has always been characterized by this "washing of feet" through "service directed in particular to the poorest and neediest" (75).

The profession of the evangelical counsels makes a person free for the service of the Gospel (n. 72). Consecrated persons have carried out innumerable apostolic works over the centuries. In undertaking such initiatives they need to pray and trust in God as if everything depends on him and to work generously as if everything depends on them (n. 73). Their active love for their brothers and sisters is founded on their love of God (n. 75). As St. Paul said, "The love of Christ impels us" (2 Cor. 5:14).

Being engaged in apostolic works "strengthens the consecrated life, gives it new enthusiasm and new motivation, and elicits faithfulness" (n. 78). While prayer is the soul of the apostolate, the apostolate animates and inspires prayer (n. 67).

Meeting the Challenges of Modern Society.

Today, as in every era, the Church faces challenges from contemporary society in the fulfillment of its mission of salvation. The worship of God has to a great extent been replaced by various types of idolatry, including what amounts to self-worship. Consecrated persons help the Church to meet today's challenges by rejecting every form of idolatry and by making God in a certain way visible to modern man.

The first challenge is that of a hedonistic culture that separates sexuality from objective moral norms, often treating it as a diversion or a consumer good. This results in an "idolatry of the sexual instinct" (n. 88). In response, consecrated persons demonstrate that it is possible to achieve self-mastery and live perfect chastity with the help of God's grace. Chastity is manifested in them as a joyful affirmation and a liberating experience (n. 88).

A second challenge is that of "a materialism which craves possessions" (n. 89). The profession of evangelical poverty attests that God is the true wealth of the human heart. It thus counteracts the "idolatry of money" so often found in modern society (n. 90).

The third challenge comes from the modern notion of freedom which is separated from objective truth and which leads to injustice and even violence. The obedience that marks the consecrated life reflects the obedience of Christ to God the Father. It testifies that there is no contradiction between obedience and freedom because obedience to God's will is the path to true human freedom (n. 91).

The Holy Father concludes the apostolic exhortation by expressing his hope that the modern world will "see in consecrated persons the joy which comes from being with the Lord" (n. 109). He calls on the Holy Trinity to bless them and give them the "grace to bring to all mankind the goodness and loving kindness of our Savior Jesus Christ" (n. 111).

Ecclesia In America
(The Church in America).
Post-Synodal Apostolic Exhortation dated
January 22, 1999.

As part of the preparation for the Great Jubilee of the Year 2000, Pope John Paul II convened five special synods of bishops to consider the situation of the Church in each of the five continents: Africa, America, Asia, Oceania, and Europe. The synods developed responses to the challenges of holiness, evangelization and service confronting the Church in each region at this milestone in history.

The special synod for America was held in Rome in 1997. The Holy Father signed the post-synodal apostolic exhortation, *Ecclesia in America,* in Mexico City in 1999. He uses the expression "America" rather than "the Americas" in the document to emphasize the need for unity and solidarity within the hemisphere. *Ecclesia in America* provides a "blueprint" or "strategic plan" for the Church in America as it enters the Third Millennium.

The subtitle of the document, *On the Encounter with the Living Jesus Christ: The Way to Conversion, Communion, and Solidarity in America,* summarizes the program for the Church prescribed by the Pope and the synod fathers. A true *encounter* with the person of the *Risen Christ* will move one to *convert* to a new life of grace and virtue. This will lead to unity or *communion* with others since sin is what divides us. Such communion will be expressed in mutual charity or *solidarity* with those around us. This in turn will draw others to an encounter with Christ thus starting the process over. In this way, a *new evangelization* of society can be achieved.

The Encounter with the Living Jesus Christ.

The starting point for evangelization is a personal encounter with our Lord who is alive and active in the Church. Such an encounter makes us aware of our calling to continue the Redeemer's mission in America. Jesus Christ is the definitive answer to the question of the meaning of life and the fundamental questions of life such as: "Where did I come from?" and "Where am I going?" (n. 10). We encounter Christ primarily in three ways: in Sacred Scripture, especially the Gospel, in the Liturgy, especially the Holy Mass and Communion, and in other people, especially the poor. As Pope Paul VI said, "On the face of every human being, especially when marked by tears and sufferings, we can and must see the face of Christ" (n. 12).

The encounter with Christ in America has been facilitated by Mary ever since she appeared to St. Juan Diego on the hill of Tepeyac in Mexico in 1531 (n. 11).

Encountering Christ in America Today.

Our apostolate takes place within the concrete situation in which we find ourselves. What especially characterizes America, the home of half of the world's Catholics? America has a Christian identity although not necessarily a Catholic identity. A distinctive feature of America is an intense popular piety that is deeply rooted in many nations. There is also a growing awareness throughout the hemisphere of the need to respect human rights.

America also has significant problems. For example, many countries are experiencing the pains of rapid urbanization, major illegal drug problems and widespread corruption in both public and private sectors. A number of countries also have significant external debt burdens.

The Path to Conversion.

Jesus calls us to repent and believe in the Good News (Mk. 1: 15). Conversion requires a change of mentality, a new mindset. "It is not simply a matter of thinking differently in the intellectual sense, but of revising the reasons behind one's actions in the light of the Gospel" (n. 26). In other words, we may need to change the *intention* behind our actions, for example, by being motivated by love of God and neighbor rather than by love of self.

Conversion must include a social dimension. It must comprehend "all aspects of life, especially those related to the social order and pursuit of the common good ... Involvement in the political field is clearly part of the vocation and activity of the lay faithful" (n. 27). In political matters a layman should be guided by his Christian conscience and accept personal responsibility for his actions and decisions. He does not act in the name of the Church.

A conversion to a new style of life requires a genuine Christian spirituality. This must be based on prayer, the Gospel and the sacraments. "Prayer holds a pre-eminent place. Prayer leads Christians ... to recognize God in every moment and in everything" (n. 29). Taking time out for prayer will make believers more conscious of the Gospel's demands and of their duties towards others. The Pope also recommends spiritual direction as a means of attaining spiritual maturity (n. 29). Knowledge of the Christian life comes chiefly from reading and reflecting on the Gospel which the faithful should do regularly (n. 31).

Conversion involves accepting the new vision which the Gospel proposes and leaving behind a *worldly* way of thinking and acting. Practicing self-denial (such as fasting) and receiving the sacrament of Penance enable a person to break bad habits and to strengthen one's will.

The Path to Communion.

Unity in the Church and among all men is a good to be achieved. "Faced with a divided world which is in search of unity, we must proclaim ... that God ... calls all people to share in [the] same Trinitarian communion ... The Church is the sign and instrument of the communion willed by God" (n. 33). Through communion with Christ, we enter into living communion with all believers. Such communion, however, requires that the deposit of faith be preserved in its purity and integrity. It cannot be compromised in the name of unity.

Communion in the Church comes from Baptism, Confirmation, and especially the Holy Eucharist. "Sharing in the Eucharist must lead to a more fervent exercise of charity" (n. 35). This insures a unity between our spiritual life and our daily life.

Unity in the Church is promoted by the bishops and priests who must avoid any involvement in politics which would necessarily be divisive (n. 39). Unity is facilitated by participation in parish life. "The parish is a privileged place where the faithful concretely experience the church" (n. 41).

In paragraph 44, the Pope provides one of his most vivid descriptions of the role of the lay faithful in the Church. It is necessary to quote this paragraph at length:

"The renewal of the Church in America will not be possible without the active presence of the laity. Therefore they are largely responsible for the future of the Church. "There are two areas in which the lay people live their vocation. The first, and the one best suited to their lay state, is the secular world, which they are called to shape, according to God's will. Their specific activity brings the Gospel to the structures of the world.

"Secularity is the true and distinctive mark of the lay person and the lay spirituality, which means that the laity strive to evangelize the various sectors of family, social, professional, cultural and political life. On a continent marked by competition and aggressiveness, unbridled consumerism and corruption, lay people are called to embody deeply evangelical values such as mercy, forgiveness, honesty, transparency of heart and patience in difficult situations. What is expected from the laity is a great creative effort in activities and works demonstrating a daily life in harmony with the Gospel. America needs lay Christians able to assume roles of leadership in society" (n. 44).

The Pope says that the second area where the laity can be involved is "intra-ecclesial" activities (e.g., assisting with parish activities). Care must be taken, however, to ensure that such work goes hand in hand with the activity of the laity in the secular sphere that cannot be undertaken by priests (n. 44).

The Path to Solidarity.

"Solidarity" is the expression of charity at the community, national and international levels. Jesus said, "Truly I say to you, as you did it to the least of my brethren, you did it to me" (Mt. 25: 40). Solidarity is a fruit of communion. We must share the spiritual and material gifts with which we have been blessed. The economic order involves not only the profit motive but also the pursuit of the common good among nations. This includes an equitable distribution of goods.

Lay people have to be trained in the Church's social doctrine so they can transform earthly realities in accordance with their faith. The Holy Father calls for the preparation of a new "Catechism of Catholic Social Doctrine" (n. 54). The Church's vision of social justice rests on the threefold foundation of "human dignity, solidarity and subsidiarity" (n. 55).

"All human rights rest on the dignity of the human person" (n. 57). The fact that man is made in the image and the likeness of God is the source of human rights and duties.

We must fight against a culture of death and the emergence of a society dominated by the powerful over the powerless including the unborn, the elderly and the incurably ill. We must commit ourselves to developing a culture of life (n. 63).

Conversion, communion and solidarity lead back to another encounter with Christ: this time one that includes an encounter with others.

The Vision of the Church in America Today: the New Evangelization.

Christ passed on to the Church the mission he had received from God the Father. The lay faithful participate in this mission. In their own way they share in the priestly, prophetic, and kingly functions of Christ (n. 66).

The vital core of the new evangelization as we enter the Third Millennium must be a clear and unequivocal proclamation of the *person* of Jesus Christ and not just a set of rules.

In caring for the poor we must not deal exclusively with their material needs, leaving them with an unsatisfied hunger for God. Our love for the poor must be preferential, but not exclusive. We cannot exclude the leaders of society from pastoral care. We must evangelize the leadership sector as well as the other sectors (n. 67).

The core of the Church's mission is a duty to lead all people to encounter Christ. "To encounter the living Christ means to accept the love by which he loves us first, to choose him, to adhere freely to his person and his plan which consists in proclaiming and bringing about the Kingdom of God" (n. 68). A true encounter with Christ will result in a burning desire to *invite others* to encounter him.

"We need to undertake an extensive catechesis using the *Catechism of the Catholic Church* which will shape the mind and touch the heart" (n. 69).

We must also evangelize the culture. "The new evangelization calls for a clearly conceived, serious and well-organized effort to evangelize culture" (n. 70). The mestiza face of Our Lady of Guadalupe is the symbol of inculturation of the Gospel, and Mary is its guiding light. Through her intercession, the Gospel will penetrate American culture. Evangelizing the media is a significant part of this process.

As we enter the Third Millennium, we must give thanks for the gift of faith that was received on the shores of America some 500 years ago. John Paul invites all Catholics in America to take an active part in the new evangelization. He especially invites Catholic families to make their homes true centers of evangelization.

The Holy Father closes the apostolic exhortation with a prayer invoking Christ who is "the way of conversion, communion and solidarity in America" (n. 76).

Pastoris Gregis
(The Shepherds of the Lord's Flock).
Post-Synodal Apostolic Exhortation dated October 16, 2003.

The 2001 Synod of Bishops considered the role of the Bishops in the Church. This post-synodal apostolic exhortation was issued by Pope John Paul II on the twenty-fifth anniversary of his election as Bishop of Rome. The subtitle of the document is *The Bishop, Servant of the Gospel of Jesus Christ for the Hope of the World.* Like Christ, a Bishop is a Good Shepherd for his flock. He is a "pastor, who, configured to Christ by his holiness of life, expends himself generously for the Church entrusted to him, while at the same time bearing in his heart a concern for all the Churches throughout the world" (n. 1).

The Synod, which took place shortly after the terrorist attacks of September 11, 2001, especially considered episcopal service in light of the theological virtue of hope (n. 2). "It is in fact the task of every Bishop to proclaim hope to the world, hope based on the proclamation of the Gospel of Jesus Christ" (n. 3). The Bishop is a "luminous sign of Christ, the Shepherd and Spouse of the Church. Acting as father, brother and friend to all, he will stand beside everyone as the living image of Christ our hope, in whom God's promises are fulfilled and all the expectations of creation are brought to completion" (n. 4).

The Mystery and Ministry of the Bishop.

Jesus chose the Twelve Apostles "to be with him" (Mk. 3: 14) and to govern the nascent Church. The mission entrusted to them is to be carried out until the end of time by their successors, the Bishops (n. 6). The Bishops carry out in an eminent and visible way the role of teacher, shepherd, and priest. They act in Christ's name as his vicars and ambassadors in exercising the functions associated with the pastoral ministry (n. 6).

The Trinity is the foundation of the episcopal ministry. The Bishop is an image of God the Father because he evokes God's paternal authority. He images God the Son, the Good Shepherd who was willing to seek out the lost sheep and bring them back to the one sheepfold. He is also an image of the Holy Spirit who by his power strengthens us in our human weakness (n. 7).

As willed by Christ himself, the episcopal ministry is collegial in nature. Like the Twelve Apostles with Peter as their head, the Bishops and the Roman Pontiff are united among themselves as a College. The College of Bishops is not an aggregate of the Bishops who govern the particular Churches. (A "particular Church" is a diocese.) Rather it is a reality that precedes the Bishops' particular offices. A Diocesan Bishop is first a member of the College of Bishops which governs the universal Church and second the head of his diocese (n. 8). The College of Bishops' supreme authority over the whole Church is solemnly exercised in Ecumenical Councils (n. 8).

The Spiritual Life of the Bishop.

A Bishop must be a man of God. In exercising his ministry, "the Bishop is called to be sanctified and to sanctify, taking as his unifying principle contemplation of the face of Christ and the proclamation of the Gospel of salvation" (n. 11). He is called to achieve holiness through the exercise of his ministry. Everything in his life is directed towards building up the life of the People of God. A Bishop, therefore, must have "an attitude of service marked by personal strength, apostolic courage and trusting abandonment to the inner working of the Spirit" (n. 11). "Unless the episcopal office is based on the witness of holiness manifested in pastoral charity, humility and simplicity of life, it ends up being reduced to a solely functional role, and, tragically, it loses its credibility before the clergy and the faithful"(n. 11).

A Bishop must cultivate a life of prayer, devoting a fair part of each day to adoration before the tabernacle (n. 16). He needs to read and meditate on the word of God and draw nourishment from the Eucharist (n. 15). He should maintain a filial devotion to Mary, the perfect teacher of the spiritual life (n. 13).

The Bishop is called to live the evangelical counsels and the Beatitudes. Because he is called to carry out faithfully the will of the Father, he must be obedient to the Gospel, the Church's tradition and the Successor of Peter (n. 19). He needs to be poor in spirit, living a life which is simple and sober, in order to make the Church the "home of the poor" (n. 20). He should provide a witness of chaste love mirroring the virginal love of Christ and has the duty to support and encourage his priests in living their commitment to celibacy (n. 21).

"In cases of grave lapses, and even more of crimes which do damage to the very witness of the Gospel, especially when these involve the Church's ministers, the Bishop must be firm and decisive, just and impartial. He is bound to intervene in a timely manner, according to the established canonical norms, for the correction and spiritual good of the sacred minister, for the reparation of scandal and the restoration of justice, and for all that is required for the protection and assistance of victims" (n. 21).

The Bishop needs ongoing formation to fulfill his pastoral responsibilities. He should participate, for example, in special courses and retreats for Bishops and undertake continual personal study (n. 24).

The ministry of Bishops is organized according to the threefold function of teaching, sanctifying and governing (n. 9).

Teacher of Faith and Herald of the Word.

The duty of proclaiming the Gospel is incumbent upon each of the Church's members but particularly upon the Bishops. "[T]he Bishop is the first preacher of the Gospel by his words and the witness of his life" (n. 26). The Bishop must reverently safeguard and courageously proclaim the faith so that his people can encounter the living person of Jesus Christ (n. 27). He will be a prophet of justice and peace and will proclaim to all the Gospel of life, truth and love (n. 67).

As authentic teachers, the Bishops are endowed with the authority of Christ himself when they teach in communion with the Roman Pontiff on matters of faith and morals. The faithful must adhere to such teaching with a religious assent of the mind (n. 29). The Bishop is ultimately in charge of the catechesis imparted in his Diocese. The basic resource for carrying out this task is the *Catechism of the Catholic Church* (n. 29). The Bishop should always work for the evangelization of culture so that the Gospel shapes the hearts and customs of the people (n. 30).

Minister of the Grace.

The Bishop is the "steward of the grace of the high priesthood" (n. 32). He carries out his ministry of sanctification "by celebrating the Eucharist and the other sacraments, by praising God in the Liturgy of the Hours, by presiding over the other sacred rites and by promoting liturgical life and authentic popular piety" (n. 33). In this way he promotes the holiness of all of the faithful. In celebrating the sacraments, the sources of divine life, he expresses the Church's "unwavering certainty of Christ's definitive victory over sin and of his coming in glory" (n. 33).

The Bishops must be vigilant in assuring that liturgical norms are always properly observed so that the beauty and dignity of the Christian liturgy will shine forth (n. 35).

Pastoral Governance.

The ministry of governance is aimed at developing in the community of the faithful the fullness of life in charity (n. 32). In exercising this ministry, the Bishops must always keep "before their eyes the example of the Good Shepherd who came not to be served but to serve and to give his life for his sheep" (cf., Mt. 20: 28, n. 42). This ministry of service finds eloquent expression in Jesus' washing the feet of the Apostles as recounted in St. John's Gospel. Jesus said to the Apostles on that occasion, "I have given you an example, that you also should do as I have done to you" (Jn. 13: 15, n. 42). Our Lord's gesture of self-giving reveals not only the meaning of the Incarnation, but also the very being of God. "God is love, and for this reason he took on the form of a servant: God put himself at the service of mankind in order to bring mankind into full communion with himself" (n. 42).

Authority in the Church is meant for the building up of the People of God. The Bishop is invested with the juridical power he needs to carry out his pastoral ministry. The task of pastoral governing demands "the ability to enter into authentic and constructive relationships with others, an aptitude for encouraging and developing cooperation, an innate goodness and patience, an understanding and compassion for those suffering in body and spirit, a spirit of tolerance and forgiveness" (n. 43).

Among the Bishop's primary duties are the spiritual care of his presbyterate and the proper formation of candidates for the priesthood (nn. 47-48).

In the Communion of the Churches.

"The universal Church is not the sum of the particular Churches or a federation of the latter" (n. 8). Rather particular Churches are "formed in the likeness of the universal Church, and in and from the particular Churches there comes into being the one and only Catholic Church" (n. 8).

All Bishops as members of the College of Bishops are obligated to be concerned about the entire Church. They have the duty to promote and defend the unity of faith and the discipline common to the whole Church (n. 55). A Diocesan Bishop is the meeting point between his particular Church and the universal Church. "The Bishop, who himself is the visible principle and foundation of unity in his own particular Church, is also the visible bond of ecclesiastical communion between his particular Church and the universal Church" (n. 55). In the universal Church, the Bishop represents his particular

Church. In his particular Church, he represents the universal Church (n. 55).

A Diocesan Bishop has a proper sphere for the independent exercise of authority that is recognized and protected by canon law. The Bishop's power coexists, however, with the supreme power of the Roman Pontiff, which is itself episcopal, ordinary and immediate over all the individual Churches and over all the pastors and faithful (n. 56). The functions of teaching and governing are thus exercised by the Diocesan Bishop in hierarchical communion with the Roman Pontiff and the College of Bishops. This does not weaken the Diocesan Bishop's authority, rather it reinforces and sustains it (n. 56).

Where will the Bishops find the resources they need to fulfill their seemingly overwhelming duties? The first resource is the special divine grace that is poured into their hearts by the Holy Spirit (cf., Rom. 5: 5, n. 73). God's love sustains them in finding the right ways to touch the hearts of men and women today. The second resource is the universal Church which is "the home and school of communion." Their communion with the College of Bishops, together with the Successor of Peter, provides them with support and solidarity. The third resource is the Bishop's own particular Church, including all of the priests, consecrated persons, pastoral workers, families and lay people, who pray for him, assist him and follow his guidance. With them he is never alone (n. 73).

In concluding the apostolic exhortation, the Holy Father urges the Bishops to become for each member of the People of God "in an outstanding and visible way, a living sign of Jesus Christ, Teacher, Priest and Pastor" (n. 74). He implores the intercession of Mary, Mother of the Church and Queen of Apostles, so that the Bishops will never fail in the task of love that Christ has entrusted to them.

Apostolic Exhortations   141

Dominicae Cenae
(On the Mystery and Worship of the Eucharist).
Apostolic Letter dated February 24, 1980.

In this apostolic letter addressed to the bishops of the Church on the occasion of Holy Thursday 1980, Pope John Paul II reflects on the Holy Eucharist, especially its liturgical aspects.

As stated by Vatican II, the Eucharist is "the source and summit of all Christian life" (n. 2). It is the source of the Church's spiritual and apostolic vitality (n. 4). John Paul says that eucharistic worship is like a "life-giving current" that links the ministerial priesthood to the common priesthood of the faithful (n. 2). In such worship the faithful adore Jesus Christ and give him thanks and praise "for having redeemed us by his death and made us sharers in immortal life through his resurrection" (n. 3).

Eucharistic devotion takes place at Holy Mass, in personal prayer before the Blessed Sacrament, at benediction of the Blessed Sacrament, in eucharistic processions, and at eucharistic congresses. The celebration of the Solemnity of the Body and Blood of Christ, which was instituted in 1264, is a special act of public worship rendered to Christ present in the Eucharist. The Holy Father encourages the faithful to deepen their eucharistic piety. "The Church and the world have a great need of eucharistic worship. Jesus waits for us in this sacrament of love. Let us be generous with our time in going to meet him in adoration and in contemplation that is full of faith and ready to make reparation for the great faults and crimes of the world. May our adoration never cease" (n. 3).

A Sign of Unity and a Bond of Charity.

As St. Paul taught, the Eucharist is a sign of unity and a bond of charity (n. 5). When we receive Holy Communion, we receive Christ himself—body, blood, soul and divinity. Our union with him associates us with all of the other members of his body which is the Church (n. 4). This is expressed, for example, in the Third Eucharistic Prayer where the Church prays, "Grant that we, who are nourished by his body and blood, may be filled with his Holy Spirit, and become one body, one spirit in Christ" (n. 9).

Our love for God and neighbor must find its source in the Blessed Sacrament. We must respond to Christ's gift of unfathomable love, which we receive in the Eucharist, with greater fraternal love for others. "Eucharistic worship is, therefore, precisely the expression of that love which is the authentic and deepest characteristic of the Christian vocation" (n. 5).

The Eucharist is a school of active love for neighbor because it shows us "what value each person, our brother or sister, has in God's eyes, if Christ offers himself equally to each one, under the species of bread and wine" (n. 6). Eucharistic worship should make us grow in awareness of the dignity of each person. This will lead us to greater love for every human being and will move us to be more forgiving and sensitive to suffering and injustice. "Since the Eucharist is the source of charity, it has always been at the center of Christ's disciples" (n. 7).

The Eucharist as a Sacrifice.

The sacredness of the Holy Sacrifice of the Mass originated in Christ's action in the Upper Room. The works and actions of the priest and the responses of the assembly echo the words and actions of Holy Thursday. "The priest offers the holy sacrifice *in persona Christi*; this means more than offering 'in the name of' or 'in the place of' Christ. *In persona* means in specific sacramental identification with Christ, the eternal High Priest, who is the author and principal subject of this sacrifice of his, a sacrifice which, in truth, nobody can take his place" (n. 8). Only Christ was able, and is able, to be the true expiation for the sins of the world.

The laity, by virtue of their common priesthood, should offer to God the Father, along with the sacrifice of Christ, their own spiritual sacrifices at the Offertory of the Mass (n. 9).

When we realize that we receive our Lord in Holy Communion, we are moved to be sorry for our sins and to desire interior purification. We must always take care that this great meeting with Christ does not become something routine, a mere habit, and that we do not receive our Lord unworthily. If we have committed a mortal sin, we must avail ourselves of the sacrament of Penance before going to Communion (n. 11).

The Eucharistic Liturgy.

The "Church has a special duty to safeguard and strengthen the sacredness of the Eucharist" (n. 8). The liturgy should be performed unhurriedly and with dignity. Where receiving Communion in the hand has been approved, pastors must be vigilant in preventing disrespect towards the eucharistic species. Those who prefer to receive the Eucharist on the tongue have a right to do so (n. 11).

The Eucharist is the greatest gift of Christ to the Church. It is the "common possession of the whole Church as a sacrament of her unity. And thus the Church has the strict duty to specify everything which concerns participation in it and its celebration" (n. 12). The bishops should insure that the directives issued by the Holy See in matters relating to the Eucharistic Mystery are followed. This will insure that the unity of which the Eucharist is a sign will be clearly manifested. Every minister of the Eucharist is also responsible for this task which is essential for the common good of the whole Church (n. 12).

The Holy Father concludes the apostolic letter by praying that the Eucharist may become an ever-greater source of life, light and unity for all members of the Church (n. 13).

Salvifici Doloris
(The Christian Meaning of Suffering).
Apostolic Letter dated February 11, 1984.

Salvifici Doloris was issued by Pope John Paul II during the Holy Year of Redemption (1983-84) which commemorated the 1950th anniversary of the Crucifixion of Christ. (The traditional date of our Lord's passion, death and resurrection is 33 A.D.) In this apostolic letter, the title to which literally means "salvific suffering," the Holy Father explains that the ultimate meaning of suffering is found in the cross of Christ. Suffering contributes to our salvation and to the salvation of all men if it is united to the cross. The Pope refers to this consoling message as the "Gospel of Suffering." As we know, he experienced a great deal of moral and physical suffering during his life.

Suffering has always been and will always be a mystery. Man is compelled to ask God the question, "Why is there suffering?" Suffering sometimes leads to a denial of God (n. 9). John Paul says that suffering is an experience of evil. In fact, in ancient Hebrew, "suffering" and "evil" were the same word (n. 7). The reality of suffering, therefore, prompts the question, "What is evil?" Christianity proclaims the essential goodness of God and of his creation. Evil is "a certain lack, limitation, or distortion of good... [Man] suffers when he 'ought' in the normal order of things to have a share in [a] good and does not have it" (n. 7).

Suffering as Punishment for Personal Sin.

The Pope provides a detailed commentary on the Book of Job which contains the most vivid expression of the problem of suffering in the Old Testament (n. 10). Job's neighbors thought that he was being punished for sins he had committed. The Old Testament shows that God does inflict suffering as a punishment for sin. In the words of the Israelites to God, "You have brought this [punishment] upon us because of our sins" (Deut. 3: 22). John Paul comments, "At the basis of human suffering, there is a complex involvement with sin" (n. 15). Punishment for sin is consistent with a conviction found in the moral conscience of humanity. "[T]he objective moral order demands punishment for transgressions, sin and crime. From this point of view, suffering appears as a 'justified evil'" (n. 10).

Another purpose of such punishment, however, is correction. "Thus, in the sufferings inflicted by God on the Chosen People, there is included an invitation to his mercy, which corrects in order to lead to conversion" (n. 12). Such punishments were not to destroy but to discipline.

Suffering thus has a meaning, not only to repay the objective evil of the sin, but also to create the possibility of moral healing. "Suffering must serve for conversion, that is, for the rebuilding of goodness in the subject who can recognize the divine mercy in this call to repentance" (n. 12). Similarly, the purpose of penance in Christian spirituality is to overcome evil and "to strengthen goodness both in man himself and in his relationship with others and especially with God" (n. 12).

The Suffering of the Innocent.

In the Book of Job, however, we see that suffering is not necessarily the result of one's own sin. Job presents the problem of the suffering of an innocent person which can draw human protest and even anguish. In Job's case, his suffering was a test of his righteousness and fidelity (n. 11).

The story of Job is a foretelling of the passion of Christ who also was innocent. To obtain a complete answer to the "why" of suffering, we must look to the revelation of divine love. The Holy Father says that "love is the fullest source of the answer to the question of the meaning of suffering" (n. 13). This answer has been given by God to man in the cross of Christ. As we read in St. John's Gospel, "For God so loved the world that he gave his only Son, that whoever believes in him should not perish but have eternal life" (Jn. 3: 16). God sent his Son so that mankind might be saved from sin and eternal death. No one has suffered more than Jesus Christ who took on the sins of all men out of love for them (n. 18).

"Salvation means liberation from evil, and for this reason it is closely bound up with the problem of suffering" (n. 14). Man "perishes" when he loses eternal life. He loses eternal life through sin. The mission of the only begotten Son was to conquer sin and death by striking at the roots of evil and thus making eternal life possible (n. 14). With Christ's victory over sin (the cause of death), the bodies and souls of the just can be reunited in the future resurrection, and they can enjoy eternal happiness in union with God (n. 15).

"In the cross of Christ not only is the Redemption accomplished through suffering, but also human suffering itself has been redeemed ... In bringing about the Redemption through suffering, Christ has also raised human suffering to the level of the Redemption (n. 19). Thus, everyone can and should be a co-Redeemer. "Each one is also called to share in that suffering through which the Redemption was accomplished" (n. 19).

Not only does Christ share in the suffering of man, man can share in the suffering of Christ (n. 20). Christ tells his followers, "If any man would come after me...let him take up his cross daily" (Lk. 9: 23). St. Paul says that whoever suffers in union with Christ, "completes what is lacking in the sufferings of Christ" (Col. 1: 24, n. 24). Uniting one's suffering to the cross will give joy because it will overcome the sense of uselessness of suffering which could otherwise consume a person interiorly and make him feel that he is only a burden to others (n. 27).

Those who share in the sufferings of Christ also share in his glory. This includes those who suffer persecution for Christ's sake as well as those who unite their personal sufferings to Christ's salvific suffering (n. 26). As St. Paul says, "The sufferings of the present time are nothing compared to the glory that will be revealed to us" (Rom. 8: 17-18, n. 22).

Caring For Those Who Suffer.

The Pope comments at length on the parable of the Good Samaritan (Lk. 10: 30-37) which he maintains is an integral part of the Gospel of Suffering (n. 28). Seeing others suffer unleashes love—the gift of self— in the human person and moves him to provide comfort. The world of human suffering calls out to the world of human love (n. 29). One cannot be a Good Samaritan unless one is capable of making a gift of self. Each of us must possess the virtue of charity so that we can be a Good Samaritan to those who are in need. "Every individual must feel as if called personally to bear witness to love in suffering" (n. 29), both individually and in union with others.

We should meditate on those words of God at the Final Judgment, "I was hungry and you gave me food, I was thirsty and you gave me drink [etc.]" (Mt. 25:34-36). Christ is unambiguously telling us how essential it is for one's eternal life to stop, as the Good Samaritan did, at the suffering of one's neighbor, have compassion and give help (n. 30). We can't excuse ourselves on the ground that we are "too busy." Making the time to help those in need is an essential step in transforming society into a "civilization of love" (n. 30).

The Holy Father summarizes the apostolic letter by saying that the meaning of suffering is both supernatural and human. It is supernatural because it is rooted in the divine mystery of Redemption. It is human because in suffering the person discovers himself, his dignity and his mission. Suffering is part of the mystery of man that takes on light in the mystery of the Incarnate Word, Jesus Christ. Through Christ the riddle of suffering and death grow meaningful. Those who suffer are not just a burden, and their lives are not useless. Such people are called to contribute to the salvation of all men (n. 31).

John Paul ends by encouraging all those who suffer. "In the terrible battle between the forces of good and evil, revealed to our eyes in the modern world, may your suffering in union with the cross of Christ be victorious!" (n. 31).

Dilecti Amici
(To the Youth of the World).
Apostolic Letter dated March 31, 1985.

This apostolic letter was written in conjunction with the United Nations International Youth Year (1985). Addressing the young people of the world with the salutation "Dear Friends," Pope John Paul II provides them with sure guidance at this critical stage in their journey through life. He begins by uniting himself to their youthful aspirations that are so full of hope. "In you there is hope, for you belong to the future, just as the future belongs to you. For hope is always linked to the future; it is the expectation of 'future good things'" (n. 1).

The Holy Father maintains that youth is a "great possession" (cf., Mk 10: 22), a special treasure that belongs not only to the young but also to all members of society. Youth is a period of special discovery about one's self and one's potential in life. It is also a time to establish a plan for one's future (n. 3).

The Question about Eternal Life.

John Paul comments at length on Christ's conversation with the rich young man recorded in the Synoptic Gospels because it addresses the questions faced by youths of every generation. When the young man asks our Lord, "Good Teacher, what must I do to inherit eternal life?" (Mk. 10: 17), he is asking in effect, "What must I do so that my life may have full value and meaning?" (n. 2). This question is particularly urgent in the time of youth when one has many options and possible paths in life.

Jesus responds to being addressed as "Good Teacher" by saying, "No one is good but God alone" (Mk. 10: 18). In this way he indicates that "only God is the ultimate basis of all values; only he gives definitive meaning to our human existence" (n. 4). If reference to God is removed from a society, the standards of morality will be lost. Evil will be put forward as a good, and good itself will be rejected. Questions about the meaning of life, truth, and good and evil, therefore, necessarily involve a reference to God. "These questions show how man without God cannot understand himself, and cannot even fulfill himself" (n. 4).

Christ is a witness to man's definitive eternal destiny in God. "I am the resurrection and the life, he who believes in me ... shall never die" (Jn. 11: 25, n. 5). Asking the question about eternal life is an indispensable part of man's search for the meaning of earthly life. "Christianity teaches us to understand temporal existence from the perspective of the Kingdom of God, from the perspective of eternal life. Without eternal life, temporal existence, however rich, however highly developed in all aspects, in the end brings man nothing other than the ineluctable necessity of death" (n. 5).

On Morality and Conscience.

Continuing his conversation with the young man, Jesus affirms the importance of observing the commandments of the Decalogue. Doing so is essential because the commandments provide an objective framework for moral behavior. Divine Revelation, including the Ten Commandments, the Beatitudes listed in the Sermon on the Mount and the "new commandment" of love, provides man with a written code of morality. The commandment of love especially opens the human person to God and neighbor. For this reason, love is the greatest and first of the commandments (n. 7).

The code of right and wrong is also inscribed in man's moral conscience. St. Paul says, "[W]hat the law requires is written on [men's] hearts while their conscience also bears witness" (Rom. 2: 15, n. 6). One must not permit the voice of conscience to be distorted or deformed by moral relativism or utilitarianism.

To "inherit eternal life" one must be "a 'person of conscience', a 'person of principles', a 'person who inspires trust'" (n. 7). Developing a moral personality is the most important contribution one can make to life in a family, a community, a professional or cultural environment or the Church (n. 7). It is also critical for attaining human maturity and authenticity.

When a Christian's life is guided by the moral law of the Gospel, he will experience true freedom. "To be truly free does not at all mean doing everything that pleases me, or doing what I want to do ... To be truly free means to use one's freedom for what is a true good ... to be truly free means to be a person of upright conscience, to be responsible, to be a person 'for others'" (n. 13).

Discovering One's Vocation.

The young man tells our Lord that he has always kept the commandments and then asks, "What do I still lack?" Jesus raises the question of vocation by replying, "If you would be perfect, go, sell what you possess and give to the poor, and you will have treasure in heaven; and come, follow me" (Mt. 19: 20-21, n. 8). Many young people receive a call to make their lives a special gift of love to God. The Holy Father says that "the Christian is capable of living in the dimension of gift" (n. 8). This may mean accepting a call to the ministerial priesthood or to the religious life. In a wider sense, however, it refers to the "life vocation" that has been entrusted to each of us by God (n. 9).

The discovery of one's life vocation is a marvelous and exciting task. One's life vocation is at the same time a "Christian vocation" because one's faith should imbue every aspect of one's life (n. 9). Since Vatican II there has been an increased awareness of the universal call to holiness and the sharing by all of the baptized in Christ's prophetic, priestly, and kingly missions. This has led to a realization that everyone must respond to the evangelical call, "Follow me." Discovering one's vocation is facilitated by spiritual direction which the Pope describes as "a systematic school of the interior life" (n. 9).

"There are different ways of becoming imitators of Christ—not only by bearing witness to the eschatological Kingdom of truth and love, but also by striving to bring about the transformation of the whole of temporal reality according to the spirit of the Gospel. It is at this point that there begins the apostolate of the laity, which is inseparable from the very essence of the Christian vocation" (n. 9). Most young people are called by God to contribute to the sanctification of the world as lay people.

The life vocation of most lay people includes marriage. When the experience of human love occurs, the Holy Father urges the young not to disfigure its beauty (n. 10). "'Blessed are the pure of heart for they shall see God' (Mt. 5: 8). [T]hrough that love that is born in you ... you must see God who is love" (n. 10). Marriage is a vocation where Christ, who gave himself for our redemption, can be imitated. "To set out on the path of the married vocation means to learn married love day by day, year by year: love according to soul and body, love that is 'patient, is kind, does not insist on its own way ... and does not rejoice at wrong': love that 'rejoices in the right,' 'love that endures all things'" (1 Cor. 13: 4-7, n. 10).

Developing One's Talents.

Youth is a time of growth. St. Luke writes, "And Jesus increased in wisdom and in stature, and in favor with God and man" (Lk. 2: 52, n. 14). Similarly, young people should grow in the possession of all that is true, good and beautiful, even if it is sometimes linked to suffering, the loss of loved ones and the experience of evil (n. 14).

Youth should include substantial contact with nature because this will facilitate absorbing "into our own human existence the very mystery of creation" (n. 14). A person also grows through his contact with others, especially friends and companions. We learn to know other human beings and develop a capacity for self-giving: for becoming men and women 'for others'" (n. 14). We also grow through contact with God. This occurs especially through prayer. If we give ourselves to God by making time for prayer, he responds by giving himself to us through grace.

During one's time in school, it is important to seek the truth about reality in its different dimensions. Jesus said, "You will know the truth and the truth will make you free" (Jn. 8: 32).

Youth is a time for discerning talents with a view to future professional work. "By the sweat of your brow you shall earn your bread" (Gen. 3: 19). "At school you have to acquire the intellectual, technical and practical skills that will enable you to take your place usefully in the great world of human work" (n. 12). Although it is usually difficult, "work in a specific way forms man, and in a certain sense creates him" (n. 12). Through work one "achieves fulfillment as a human being" (n. 12).

Future Leaders of the World.

"You young people are the hope of the Church" (n. 15). Today's youth are facing a world filled with tensions and threats "on a scale never before known in the history of humanity" (n. 15). For the answers to the world's problems, the Holy Father urges them to look to the Gospel of Christ. "And this is the victory that overcomes the world, our faith" (1 Jn. 5: 4, n. 15).

The young naturally desire genuine brotherhood among all people. There can be brothers and sisters, however, only where there is a Father. "Accepting God's fatherhood can lead human hearts away from enmity, hatred, violence, terrorism, discrimination— from the situations in which human dignity and human rights are trampled upon" (n. 15). John Paul urges young people to persevere in the struggle against evil and the Evil One. If the word of God abides in them, they will gradually succeed in "changing the world, transforming it, making it more human, more fraternal—and at the same time more of God" (n. 15).

The Holy Father's parting words to the youth of the world echo Mary's words to the stewards at the wedding feast at Cana, "Do whatever Christ tells you" (n. 16).

Mulieris Dignitatem
(On the Dignity and Vocation of Woman).
Apostolic Letter dated August 15, 1988.

In *Mulieris Dignitatem*, which was issued during the Marian Year 1987-88, Pope John Paul II reflects on the greatness and dignity of the vocation of woman. The Holy Father says that this must be understood before one can speak of the proper role of women in the Church and in society. In a word, the *dignity* of woman is based on her call to eternal union with God as a person made in God's image. The special *vocation* of woman is to welcome and care for human life.

The Pope begins the apostolic letter by referring to the Blessed Virgin Mary as the model of woman as willed by God. He quotes St. Paul's Letter to the Galatians, "When the fullness of time came, God sent forth his son, born of woman" (Gal. 4: 4). A woman is thus found at the center of the Incarnation, the greatest event in human history (n. 3).

In Mary, who is "full of grace," we find the fullness of perfection. Mary teaches us that "to serve ... means to reign" (n. 5). By agreeing to become the Handmaid of the Lord, she became the Queen of Heaven. Jesus and Mary "show all people the royal dignity of service, the dignity which is joined in the closest possible way to the vocation of every person" (n. 5).

How Man and Woman Reflect the Image and Likeness of God.

We read in Genesis 1: 27, "God created man in his own image ... male and female he created them." This passage indicates that men and women are essentially equal from the standpoint of their humanity. While the human creature is "like God" in that he or she has a rational nature, John Paul maintains that man and woman reflect "the image and likeness of God" much more in their reciprocity than as individuals (n. 6). This is because man and woman, through their intimate love as husband and wife, are called to mirror in the world the love of the three divine Persons for each other in the intimate mystery of the one divine life (cf., n. 7).

"Man and woman are called from the beginning not only to exist 'side by side' or 'together,' but they are also called to exist mutually 'one for the other'" (n. 7). Thus God intended man and woman to be able to exist in a "unity of the two."

Unfortunately, sin entered the world and destroyed the original unity that man and woman enjoyed in the state of original justice. Sin not only damaged man's union with God and with the external world, it also damaged the relationship between man and woman as a community of persons (n. 9). Instead of a "unity of the two," mankind began to experience the domination of man over woman. "He shall rule over you" (Gen. 3: 16, n. 10). Such domination, an effect of sin, resulted in the loss of the fundamental equality of man and woman to the detriment of both, but especially to the detriment of women.

An authentic marital union requires the husband and the wife to be treated as equal subjects in accordance with their status as spiritual persons. The disorder caused by sin must be overcome so that women are not treated as objects of "domination"and "male possession." Overcoming this evil inheritance is the task of every human being. Whenever a man is responsible for offending a woman's personal dignity, he acts contrary to his own dignity as well (n. 10). The Holy Father challenges men to look within themselves to see if they are treating women, especially their wives, as objects rather than as persons (n. 14).

Women in the Gospel.

Jesus Christ was a promoter of women's true dignity and vocation. "Within Christianity, more than in any other religion and since its very beginning, women have had a special dignity" (n. 1). By re-establishing the indissolubility of marriage, Christ greatly improved the status and well-being of women. "Moses allowed you to divorce your wives, but from the beginning it was not so" (Mt. 19: 8, n. 12). Christ's words and deeds always expressed the respect and honor due to women. The Pope points out that this clearly constituted an innovation with respect to the prevailing customs of the time (n. 13).

There are many occasions in the Gospel where our Lord dealt with women. For example, one of the most important of Christ's recorded conversations was with Martha when he said: "I am the resurrection and the life, he who believes in me ... shall never die" (Jn. 11: 21-27, n. 15). The presence of the women at the foot of the cross demonstrated that, in this ultimate test of fidelity, the women proved stronger than the Apostles. Their great love overcame their fear (n. 15). Jesus seemed to reward the women by allowing them be the first at the tomb to discover his resurrection (n. 16).

Two Dimensions of Woman's Vocation.

Virginity and motherhood are two dimensions of the fulfillment of the female personality. Their full meaning is seen in Mary, who as a Virgin became the Mother of the Son of God (n. 17). As such, she is able to love God as a virgin and humanity as a mother.

In motherhood, women participate in the great mystery of eternal generation. While both spouses share in the creative power of God in bringing new human life into existence, the mother's role is special (n. 18). Bearing and raising children literally absorb the energies of her body and soul. The man must be fully aware that he owes a special debt to the woman. No program of equal rights is valid unless it takes the demands of motherhood into account (n. 18).

Celibacy for the kingdom of heaven is a vocation that results from a special grace on the part of God. It is a special form of spousal love that is "a way to devote all of the energies of the body and soul during one's earthly life exclusively for the sake of the eschatological kingdom" (n. 20).

Both marriage and apostolic celibacy signify a sincere gift of the person and point to the ultimate calling of the human creature to eternal happiness in communion with the three divine Persons (n. 21).

Ephesians, Chapter 5.

One of the more controversial passages in the New Testament is: "Wives, be subject to your husbands as to the Lord. For the husband is the head of the wife, even as Christ is the head of the Church" (Eph. 5: 22-23, n. 24). The Pope maintains that this passage must be understood in the context of the *mutual* subjection of the spouses called for in the often ignored preceding verse: "Be subject to one another out of reverence for Christ" (Eph. 5: 21). The requirement of mutual subjection prevents the statement "Wives, be subject to your husbands" from implying that husbands need not be subject to their wives or that wives must obey their husbands as servants. The necessity of mutual subjection in marriage is supported by the subsequent verse: "Husbands, love your wives, as Christ loved the Church and gave himself up for her" (Eph. 5: 25). This verse clearly affirms the woman's status as a subject and as an equal partner in the marriage (n. 24). If spousal love finds its true source in Christ, the husband and the wife will be united in perfect harmony.

The radical equality of man and woman and husband and wife is a Gospel innovation that is still being learned after two millennia of Christianity. "[T]he awareness that in marriage there is a mutual 'subjection of the spouses out of reverence for Christ', and not just that of the wife to the husband, must gradually establish itself in hearts, consciences, behavior and customs" (n. 24). To those who might ask why this process has taken so long, John Paul asks in return, how many generations were required for the abolition of slavery? How many forms of slavery have yet to disappear? (n. 24).

The "Royal Priesthood."

While women are not members of the ministerial priesthood, they do share in the common priesthood of the faithful. "In calling only men as his apostles, Christ acted in a completely free and sovereign manner" (n. 26). Perhaps one reason why Christ desired that priests be male is that the priest acts *in persona Christi* in celebrating the Eucharist. Because the Eucharist expresses the redemptive act of Christ, the Bridegroom, towards the Church, the

Bride, this mystery is best represented when performed by a man (n. 26).

In any case, a person's contribution to the Church ultimately depends on his or her holiness rather than on the performance of any particular task. The holiest person in the Church is Mary, who is not a priest. The Holy Father cites many women who enriched the Church by fulfilling their vocation to holiness and who thus exemplified the "royal priesthood" of Christ (1 Pet. 2: 9, nn. 27-30).

The Feminine Genius.

"When the author of the Letter to the Ephesians calls Christ 'the Bridegroom' and the Church 'the Bride,' he indirectly confirms through this analogy the truth about woman as bride. The Bridegroom is the one who loves. The Bride is loved: it is she who receives love, in order to love in return" (n. 29).

The dignity of woman is measured by the order of love. It is closely connected with the love she receives and the love she gives in return. Woman can only find herself by giving love to others (n. 30).

God entrusts the human being to woman in a special way. The moral force of a woman draws strength from her awareness of this entrusting (n. 30). The genius of woman is her ability to love that is expressed through her gift for giving birth to, welcoming, and caring for human life.

The Pope ends the apostolic letter by thanking God for each and every woman and for all of the "great works of God" that have been accomplished through them (n. 31).

Tertio Millennio Adveniente
(As the Third Millennium Draws Near).
Apostolic Letter dated November 14, 1994.

"When the fullness of time had come, God sent forth his Son, born of women" (Gal. 4: 4, n. 1). With these words of St. Paul, Pope John Paul II begins this apostolic letter on preparing for the Great Jubilee of the Year 2000. In his first encyclical he said that his pontificate would be like a "new Advent" leading up to the year 2000 (n. 23). In this letter, the Holy Father provides the faithful with a detailed explanation of the meaning of the Jubilee and prescribes specific preparations for it.

The Pope summarizes the purpose of the Jubilee celebration by saying that it should "confirm the Christians of today in their *faith* in God who revealed himself in Christ, sustain the *hope* which reaches out in expectation of eternal life and rekindle their *charity* in active service to their brothers and sisters" (n. 31, emphasis added). A jubilee is an occasion of special grace and joy. The Holy Father expresses his desire that the Great Jubilee will be an extended prayer of praise and thanksgiving "especially for the gift of the incarnation of the Son of God and of the redemption which he accomplished" (n. 32).

The Holy Father intended the Jubilee to be an opportunity to reflect on the whole of Christian history which he says "appears to us as a single river into which many tributaries pour their waters. The year 2000 invites us to gather with renewed fidelity and ever deeper communion along the banks of this great river: the river of revelation, of Christianity and the Church, a river which flows through human history starting from the event which took place at Nazareth and then at Bethlehem 2,000 years ago" (n. 25).

"Jesus Christ is the Same Yesterday and Today" (Heb. 13: 8).

As we read in St. John's Gospel, "[T]he Word became flesh and dwelt amongst us" (Jn. 1: 14, n. 3). In the fullness of time the eternal Word took on the condition of a creature. Jesus was born of the Chosen People in fulfillment of the promises made to Abraham and repeated to the prophets. Unlike the prophets who spoke in God's name, Jesus *is* God who speaks in his own name (n. 6).

Christianity is essentially different from all other religions because, while other religions are about *man seeking God*, Christianity is about *God seeking man*. In Christianity, with its starting point in the Incarnation of the Word, God "comes in person to speak to man himself and to show him the path by which he may be reached" (n. 6). "In Christ, religion is no longer a 'blind search for God' but the response of faith to God who reveals himself. It is a response in which man speaks to God as his Creator and Father" (n. 6).

"In Jesus Christ God not only speaks to man but also seeks him out. The Incarnation of the Son of God attests that God goes in search of man" (n. 7). God is thus like the shepherd who searches out the lost sheep. God does this because of his love for man: "For God so loved the world that he gave his only-begotten Son, so that those who believe in him might not perish but may have life everlasting" (Jn. 3: 16). God needed to do this because man had turned away from him and followed the path of evil. God seeks to bring man back to the path of holiness. "Overcoming evil: This is the meaning of the Redemption" (n. 7).

Evil was overcome by the passion and death of Christ who redeemed man's debt of sin and reconciled him to God.

Christianity is "the religion of 'dwelling in the heart of God,' of sharing in God's very life" (n. 8). Revelation speaks of a fulfillment which man is called to achieve in the course of his earthly life. "Man achieves this fulfillment of his destiny through the sincere gift of self, a gift which is made possible only through the encounter with God. It is in God that man finds full self-realization: this is the truth revealed by Christ. Man fulfills himself in God, who comes to meet him through his eternal Son" (n. 9).

The Jubilee of the Year 2000.

A jubilee is a "special year of the Lord's favor" (Is. 61: 2). The custom of celebrating jubilees, which began in the Old Testament, has been continued in the Catholic Church. As we read in Leviticus, "You shall hallow the 50th year and proclaim liberty throughout the land to all its inhabitants; it shall be a jubilee for you, when each of you shall return to his property and each of you shall return to his family" (Lev. 25: 10, n. 12).

Emancipation from debt and slavery was an important feature of a jubilee year in the Old Testament. It foretold the freedom that would one day be won by the Messiah. For the Church, the jubilee is a special time of remission from sin and reconciliation with God and neighbor. During a jubilee year, the Church grants special indulgences that remit the temporal punishment due to sin (n. 14). As the term "jubilee" implies, the year is a special time of joy—both the inner joy that accompanies personal conversion and forgiveness of sin and the joy of outward celebrations with others (n. 16).

Preparation for the Great Jubilee.

The preparation for the Great Jubilee began with the Second Vatican Council which marked the beginning of a new era in the life of the Church. The Holy Father calls for a renewed commitment to apply the teachings of Vatican II to the life of each individual and of the whole Church (n. 20). Such a commitment is necessary for there to be a "new springtime of Christian life" (n. 18).

The Synods of Bishops that have been held since Vatican II, including the five continental synods specifically held in anticipation of the Jubilee, have prepared the Church for the year 2000 by promoting a "new evangelization" (n. 21). They have emphasized the importance of the entire people of God sharing in Christ's mission as prophet, priest and king.

Another element of preparation was the Marian Year 1987–88 which drew attention to the presence of the Mother of God in the mystery of Christ and the Church (n. 26).

Immediate Preparation.

After consulting with the members of the College of Cardinals who met in Rome in 1994, the Holy Father prescribed a two-stage program of preparation for the final years before for the Jubilee. The first stage (1994–96) promoted in the Christian people an awareness of the value and meaning of the Jubilee. The second stage (1997–99) focused on the three Persons of the Blessed Trinity.

The first year of immediate preparation (1997) was centered on Jesus Christ, the one Savior of the world. The second year (1998) was focused on the Holy Spirit, the Sanctifier of Christ's disciples. The third year (1999) was centered on God the Father and his unconditional love for every human creature. The chart below that summarizes the Holy Father's indications for the three years of immediate preparation.

The Pope provided that the celebration of the Great Jubilee would take place simultaneously in the Holy Land, in Rome and in the local Churches throughout the world. He sought to insure that the celebration would give glory to the Trinity "from whom everything in the world and in history comes and to whom everything returns" (n. 55). An International Eucharistic Congress was held during the year 2000 in accordance with the Jubilee's "intensely eucharistic" spirit (n. 55). "[I]n the sacrament of the Eucharist the Savior, who took flesh in Mary's womb 20 centuries ago, continues to offer himself to humanity as the source of divine life" (n. 55).

"Jesus Christ is the Same ... Forever" (Heb. 13:8).

The Holy Father concludes the apostolic letter by noting that, like the mustard seed in the Gospel, the Church "has grown and become like a great tree, able to cover the whole of humanity with her branches" (n. 56). The Church must continue to grow so that all people may belong to the People of God. As reiterated by Vatican II, the whole of mankind is called by the grace of God to salvation.

The Pope entrusts the Great Jubilee to Mary, the Mother of Fairest Love, praying, "May the unassuming young women of Nazareth who 2,000 years ago offered to the world the incarnate Word, lead the men and women of the new millennium toward the one who is 'the true light that enlightens every man'" (Jn. 1:9, n. 59).

Immediate Preparation
for the
Great Jubilee of the Year 2000

Year:	1997	1998	1999
Divine Person:	Jesus Christ	Holy Spirit	God the Father
Theme:	Jesus Christ: the One Savior of the World	The Holy Spirit: Sanctifier of Christ's Disciples	God the Father: his Unconditional Love for every Human Creature.
Focus:	Preaching the Good News	Sanctification through Grace	Conversion from Sin
Theological Virtue:	Faith	Hope	Charity
Sacrament:	Baptism	Confirmation	Penance
Unity:	With other Christians	In the Church	With non-Christians
Mary:	Mother of God the Son, Model of Faith	Spouse of God the Holy Spirit, Model of Hope	Daughter of God the Father, Model of Charity

Dies Domini
(On Keeping the Lord's Day Holy).
Apostolic Letter dated May 31, 1998.

In this apostolic letter Pope John Paul II explains why Sunday is a special day of faith, why the faithful must participate in the Eucharistic celebration on Sunday, and how the faithful must celebrate Sunday as a day of joy, rest and solidarity.

In apostolic times, Sunday was called the "Lord's day" ("Domingo" in Spanish) because of its close connection with the core of the Christian mystery. Sunday has lost much of its special character in modern society. It is often treated as just part of the weekend—a time to relax and catch up. The Pope reminds us that it must be much more than this. It is a Christian's duty to keep Sunday holy. "Do not be afraid to give your time to Christ," he says, "Time given to Christ is never lost" (n. 7).

Sunday has five meanings for a Christian. It commemorates the day of the week on which God rested from his work of creation, the day the Hebrews were liberated from Egypt (Passover), the day on which Christ rose from the dead (Easter), the day on which the Holy Spirit descended on the apostles (Pentecost), and the "eighth day" which symbolizes eternity. Each meaning is enough for a celebration. All five add up to a very special cause for celebration indeed.

The Celebration of the Creator's Work.

In Genesis we read that God made the world in six days and rested on the seventh. On seeing that creation was good, "he blessed the seventh day and made it holy" (Gen. 2, 3). Thus the seventh day (the "Sabbath" in Hebrew) is the day of the Creator's joyful rest.

The work of creation continues with man as a co-worker with God. (The Holy Father referred to this in *Laborem Exercens* as the "Gospel of Work.") Like God, we should work six days but rest on the seventh to contemplate the goodness of creation and to give thanks and praise to the Creator. Observing the Sabbath as a day of rest and interrupting the rhythm of work expresses man's dependence on God and affirms the fact that everything belongs to God, even time. Without a frequent reminder of this truth, man would risk not being a co-worker with the Creator. He would risk working with an egotistical intention instead.

In the Old Testament, the order of creation is linked with the order of salvation. The observance of the Sabbath is associated with the liberation of the Israelites from the slavery of the Egyptians which took place on that day. This commemoration is so important that the Sabbath precept is contained in the Ten Commandments. "Remember the Sabbath and keep it holy" (Ex. 20: 8). Observing the Third Commandment is not just a matter of discipline. It is a fundamental expression of man's relationship with God. This relationship demands that man set aside certain times for prayer. The Sabbath is the day *par excellence* for such prayer.

In the New Testament the meaning of the Sabbath has been transferred to Sunday because the Resurrection of Christ both revealed the mystery of creation and accomplished mankind's liberation from the slavery of sin. The spiritual meaning of the Sabbath is thus fully realized in the Resurrection of our Lord on Easter Sunday.

The Day of the Risen Lord and the Gift of the Holy Spirit.

Sunday, the first day of the week in the Roman calendar ("Primeiro" in Portuguese), is the Day of the Risen Lord. It should be commemorated as a weekly Easter. In fact in Russian the word for "Sunday" is the word for "resurrection." We know that our Lord appeared to the disciples on Easter evening and on the next Sunday. He may have continued appearing to them on each Sunday until his Ascension to establish the custom of the Sunday assembly of the faithful. In any case we know that Christians began to assemble on that day. The Greek word for "assembly" (*ecclesia*) is the origin of the English word "church." Since Sunday was a workday in the Roman Empire, the first Christians had to meet for worship before sunrise according to the Roman historian, Pliny the Younger.

Where the first day of the week is denominated as the "day of the sun" (e.g., in English and German speaking countries), this can be a reminder that Christ is the light of the world. It also evokes the first day of creation on which God said, "Let there be light" (Gen. 1, 3).

The sun as fire is imagery of the Holy Spirit. Pentecost also took place on a Sunday. "The weekly Easter is also a weekly Pentecost when Christians relive the Apostles' joyful encounter with the Risen Lord and receive the life-giving breath of his Spirit" (n. 28).

The "eighth day" symbolized eternity in the Old Testament. It is a day beyond the seven-day week, a day without end. St. Augustine said that, in celebrating Sunday both as the "first" day and as the "eighth" day, the Christian is reminded that his ultimate goal is eternal life (n. 26).

Given all of these dimensions, Sunday is the supreme day of faith. The celebration of Sunday, therefore, is an indispensable element of the Christian identity.

The Eucharistic Assembly as the Heart of Sunday.

On Sunday, the Church celebrates the living presence of the Risen Lord. "[I]t is not enough that the disciples of Christ pray individually ... [Christians] are not saved as individuals alone, but as members of the Mystical Body. ... It is important, therefore, that they come together [to demonstrate that they are] 'one' in Christ" (n. 31). In the Sunday assembly their unity becomes visible. As stated in the *Catechism of the Catholic Church*, "The Sunday celebration of the Lord's Day and his Eucharist is at the heart of the Church's life" (n. 32).

At Sunday Mass, Christians relive the experience of the apostles when they were gathered together with the Lord on Easter evening. At the Eucharistic celebration, they encounter the Risen Christ at the table of the Word and the table of the Bread of Life. They hear the word of God and receive Jesus Christ "body, blood, soul and divinity." In the Mass all of the faithful participate in the priestly mission of Christ by offering their prayers, works, joys and sufferings to the Father along with the Sacred Victim. Thus the Pope says, "the sacrifice of Christ becomes also the sacrifice of the members of his Body" (n. 43).

The Eucharistic gathering is also a special experience of brotherhood among the faithful. They must first be reconciled with their brothers and sisters before they can offer their gifts at the altar (n. 44).

The Holy Father describes how the obligation to attend Mass on Sunday developed. He points out that many Christians were martyred for attending Mass at a time when it was not an obligation. In the 1917 *Code of Canon Law* this obligation first became a universal law of the Church. It is also contained in the 1983 *Code of Canon Law* as follows: "Those who deliberately fail in this obligation commit a grave sin" (Canon 2181).

Sunday as a Day of Joy, Rest and Solidarity.

The obligation to keep Sunday holy extends beyond attending Mass. On Sunday the whole day must be an active remembrance of God's saving work. Christians must live Sunday in a way consistent with the peace and joy of the Risen Lord (n. 52).

Sunday, the weekly Easter, should be celebrated above all as a day of joy. Pope Paul VI said, "Christian joy is the sharing in the unfathomable joy, at once divine and human, found in the heart of the glorified Christ" (n. 58). To experience this joy, we need periodic rest from our work. "Six days you shall labor … but the seventh is the Sabbath … You shall do no work" (Deut. 5, 12-15). In honoring God's rest, man fully discovers himself (n. 61).

The Edict of Constantine (July 3, 321), which made Sunday a legal holiday in the Roman Empire, facilitated Sunday worship. Constantine was the first Christian Roman emperor. The Church forbade "servile" work to prevent masters from requiring their servants/slaves to work on Sunday. Thus the Sunday rest was established as a worker's right. We should not make others work unnecessarily on Sunday.

The Pope paraphrases Canon 1247 of the *Code of Canon Law* when he says, "Christians…are obligated in conscience to arrange their Sunday rest in a way that allows them to take part in the Eucharist, refraining from work and activities which are incompatible with the sanctification of the Lord's Day, with its characteristic joy and necessary rest for body and spirit" (n. 67).

Sunday should be a day of special family life. "Through Sunday rest we see the true face of the people with whom we live" (n. 67). The beauties of nature can also be rediscovered and enjoyed. Sunday is a day that man can be at peace with God, with himself and with others.

Such rest should not, however, be emptiness or boredom. It must offer spiritual enrichment, contemplation and fraternity. Sunday can be devoted to works of mercy, charity and apostolate. "Since apostolic times, Sunday has been for Christians a moment of fraternal sharing with the poor" (n. 70). If Sunday is a day of joy, Christians should declare by their behavior that they cannot be happy "on their own." They must look for people who need their help: the sick, the suffering, the lonely, the elderly, orphans, immigrants, etc. Our Lord's healing on the Sabbath was consistent with this meaning.

Conclusion.

Keeping Sunday holy is an important witness Christians are called to bear. It is not only an obligation but also a need arising from the depths of the Christian life.

Ensuring the value of this sacred day will bear rich fruit in Christian communities and will have a positive influence in civil society as well. "It will make Christ's disciples more effective in building the civilization of love" (n. 87).

In summary, on Sunday we must thank God for his creation, we must thank Christ for liberating us from sin, and we must remember that everything belongs to God, including time.

Novo Millennio Ineunte
(At the Beginning of the New Millennium).
Apostolic Letter dated January 6, 2001.

This apostolic letter was signed by Pope John Paul II immediately after he closed the Holy Door on the last day of the Great Jubilee of the Year 2000. In it he looks back on the events of the Holy Year and ahead to the apostolic tasks awaiting the Church as she enters the Third Millennium. The Pope begins the document by recalling the words of Jesus to St. Peter: "'Put out into the deep' for a catch: *Duc in Altum* (Lk. 5: 4). Peter and his first companions trusted Christ's words and cast the nets. 'When they had done this, they caught a great number of fish' (Lk. 5: 6)" (n. 1). Christ tells the disciples that henceforth they will be catching men (Lk. 5: 10). John Paul similarly challenges the faithful to take up the Church's evangelizing mission with fresh enthusiasm. He reminds us that, to be effective in this task, we must strive for holiness, practice charity and collaborate with others.

Meeting Christ: the Legacy of the Great Jubilee.

The Holy Father gives thanks to God for the many graces and blessings bestowed on the Church during the worldwide celebration of the Jubilee. It demonstrated that the Gospel message is as fresh today as it was 2,000 years ago (n. 4). Millions of people visited Rome from all over the world and from all walks of life. They ranged "from old people to the sick and handicapped, from workers in factories and fields to sports people, from artists to university teachers, from bishops and priests to people in consecrated life, from politicians to journalists, to the military personnel who came to confirm the meaning of their service as a service of peace" (n. 10).

The Pope recalls some of the unforgettable events of the Jubilee such as his pilgrimage to the Holy Land, the International Eucharistic Congress, and World Youth Day when he met with some two million young people in the fields of Tor Vergata. What he says about the young applies to people of all ages: "If Christ is presented to young people as he really is, they experience him as an answer that is convincing and they can accept his message, even when it is demanding and bears the mark of the cross" (n. 9).

The core of the great legacy of the Jubilee is the "*contemplation of the face of Christ:* Christ considered in his historical features and in his mystery, Christ known through his manifold presence in the Church and in the world, and confessed as the meaning of history and the light of life's journey" (n. 15). The special encounter with Jesus Christ that we experienced during the Jubilee has strengthened us for the tasks that lay ahead.

A Face to Contemplate.

We can contemplate the *human* face of Christ through the eye-witness accounts of his life contained in the New Testament. They provide us with a vision of faith based on precise historical testimony (n. 17). We see Jesus born in a stable in Bethlehem, growing up and working as a carpenter in Nazareth and conducting his public ministry throughout Palestine. After God the Father revealed the divinity of Jesus to the disciples, Peter is able to proclaim by faith, "You are the Christ, the Son of the living God" (Mt. 16: 16, n. 19).

Christ's identity is to be found in the intimate and inseparable union of his divinity and his humanity. Jesus is true God and true man: "one person in two natures" (n. 21). He is "the new man" who calls redeemed humanity to share his divine life. "[I]t is only because the Son of God truly became man that man, in him and through him, can truly become a child of God" (n. 23).

A paradoxical aspect of the mystery of Christ is confronted when he is seen on the cross (n. 25). Through his passion and death, Christ simultaneously experienced the profound joy of unity with God the Father and the unspeakable agony that ended with a final cry of abandonment. Contemplating the *bleeding* face of Christ teaches us that bliss and pain are always blended for human creatures who seek holiness during their earthly pilgrimage (n. 27).

Finally, the Church contemplates the *glorious* face of the Risen Christ. Through his victory over death, "he became the source of eternal salvation to all who obey him" (1 Cor. 5: 7-9, n. 28). He "is the same yesterday, today and forever" (Heb. 13: 8, n. 28).

Starting Afresh from Christ.

Our faith has been strengthened by the renewed assurance gained during the Jubilee that Christ is with us. Looking ahead, we must ask ourselves, "What must we do as followers of Christ? What is God expecting of us?" While urging the faithful to make a fresh start, the Pope prescribes the same spiritual program that has always been lived in the Church. "Ultimately, it has its center in Christ himself, who is to be known, loved and imitated, so that in him we may live the life of the Trinity, and with him transform history until its fulfillment in the heavenly Jerusalem" (n. 29).

Pastoral initiatives for spiritual progress must above all be aimed at increasing the personal holiness of the faithful (n. 30). We must take seriously the "universal call to holiness" proclaimed by Vatican II. Holiness is both a *gift* that is offered in Baptism and a *task* that must shape the whole of Christian life: "This is the will of God, your sanctification" (1 Thess. 4: 3). "All the Christian faithful, of whatever state or rank, are called to the fullness of the Christian life and to the perfection of charity" (n. 30). No Christian can "settle for a life of mediocrity, marked by a minimalist ethic and a shallow religiosity" (n. 31). Rather, each one must strive to "Be perfect as your heavenly Father is perfect" (Mt. 5: 48, n. 31).

The Holy Father thanks the Lord for having been able to beatify and canonize during his pontificate "many lay people who attained holiness in the most ordinary circumstances of life. The time has come to re-propose wholeheartedly to everyone this high standard of ordinary Christian living" (n. 31).

Attaining personal holiness requires genuine "*training in holiness.*" An important aspect of such spiritual training is learning to pray. "Prayer develops that conversation with Christ which makes us his intimate friends. 'Abide in me and I in you' (Jn. 15: 4). This reciprocity is the very substance and soul of the Christian life" (n. 33). Prayer is a genuine dialogue of love sustained by grace. Christian communities must be "*schools of prayer*" which teach that a meeting with Christ is expressed not only in petition, but also in thanksgiving, praise and adoration until the heart truly "falls in love" with him (n. 33).

Training in holiness also requires participation in the liturgy and reception of the sacraments. Sunday must be observed as a "true weekly Easter" in which our Lord's Resurrection is remembered and the Eucharist is shared (n. 35). Sacramental confession is "the ordinary way of obtaining the forgiveness and the remission of serious sins committed after Baptism" (n. 37). While the Jubilee Year witnessed a return to the sacrament of Penance, pastors must continue to make an effort to present it to the faithful with courage, confidence and perseverance (n. 37).

Our spiritual exercises should also include listening to the word of God. Sacred Scripture should be studied by all, including the laity (n. 39).

By opening our hearts to the love of God, such spiritual training will enable us to love our neighbors and shape history according to God's plan (n. 33).

Witness to Love.

"By this all will know that you are my disciples, that you have love for one another" (Jn. 13: 35, n. 42). Habitual love for each other, which the Holy Father calls the "*domain of communion*," embodies the very essence of the mystery of the Church. Christ tells us, "Love one another as I have loved you" (Jn. 13: 34). The Church must be a "*school of communion*" which teaches the faithful how to love. We must attend to the needs of those around us, who are our brothers and sisters in Christ, and offer them deep and genuine friendship. We must learn to "make room" for them, bearing "each other's burdens" (Gal. 6: 2, n. 43).

A spirituality of communion is also manifested in compassionate care for the poor. This includes the materially poor, such as those suffering from hunger, illiteracy or a lack of shelter or medical care, and the spiritually poor, often found in affluent societies, who are threatened by despair at the lack of meaning in their lives, drug addiction, abandonment in sickness or old age or social discrimination (n. 50).

The Church's communion with mankind is expressed in her social doctrine, including her insistence on the respect for the life of every human being from conception until natural death. Applying such doctrine to the structures of society "is not a case of imposing on non-believers a vision based on faith, but [rather] of interpreting and defending the values rooted in the very nature of the human person" (n. 51). It is a true work of charity.

The lay faithful must be involved in matters affecting culture, politics, the economy and the family to insure that the fundamental principles of morality are respected in these areas which shape our civilization (n. 51). The Pope reminds the laity that they have a specific vocation to "seek the kingdom of God by engaging in temporal affairs and ordering them according to the plan of God" (n. 46).

In carrying out a "new evangelization," we should not fear that sharing our faith will offend the identity of members of other cultures or traditions. The proclamation of Christ is "a gift meant for all and to be offered to all with the greatest respect for the freedom of each one" (n. 56).

John Paul urges the faithful to study the documents of Vatican II which was "the great grace bestowed on the Church in the twentieth century" and which will be a sure compass to guide us in the century now beginning (n. 57).

Duc in Altum!

The Holy Father concludes the apostolic letter by comparing the new millennium to "a vast ocean upon which we shall venture, relying on the help of Christ" (n. 58). We should undertake our apostolic mandate with the enthusiasm of the first Christians. On this journey of faith we will be accompanied by the Blessed Virgin Mary, the "Star of the New Evangelization" (n. 58). She is the radiant dawn who will guide our steps as we enter the new millennium.

Rosarium Virginis Mariae
(The Rosary of the Virgin Mary).
Apostolic Letter dated October 16, 2002.

In this apostolic letter issued on the commencement of the twenty-fifth year of his pontificate, Pope John Paul II reflects on the Rosary which he describes as his "favorite prayer" (n. 2). He invites the faithful to pray the Rosary as a way to "*contemplate with Mary the face of Christ*" (n. 3). Such contemplation is essential for one to attain genuine holiness. In order to revitalize this devotion, the Holy Father proclaimed the year from October 2002 to October 2003 as "*the Year of the Rosary*" (n. 3).

Contemplating Christ with Mary.

The Gospel scene of Christ's Transfiguration (Mt. 17: 2) can be seen as "*an icon of Christian contemplation*" (n. 9). "To look upon the face of Christ, to recognize its mystery amid the daily events and the sufferings of human life, and then to grasp the divine splendor definitively revealed in the Risen Lord, seated in glory at the right hand of the Father: this is the task of every follower of Christ and therefore of each one of us" (n. 9).

Our primary model for contemplating Christ is Mary. Pope Paul VI said that the recitation of the Rosary helps "the individual to meditate on the mysteries of the Lord's life as seen through the eyes of her who was closest to the Lord" (n. 12). Because no one knows Christ better than Mary, no one can better introduce us to a profound knowledge of his mystery.

Christian spirituality requires the disciple "to become conformed ever more fully to his Master"

(n. 15). That is, his or her thoughts, words and deeds should be ever more Christ-like. In order to "put on the Lord Jesus Christ" (Rom. 13: 14), however, one must know him and be his friend. Devotion to Mary helps us to be conformed to Christ because her life is deeply joined to his. "Mary lives only in Christ and for Christ" (n. 15).

The Mysteries of the Rosary.

The Rosary is a "compendium of the Gospel" because it conveys the depth of the Gospel message through the contemplation of the key Christian mysteries. To bring out more fully the Christological depth of the Rosary, the Holy Father broadens it to include mysteries associated with Christ's public ministry. He calls these mysteries the "mysteries of light" or the "luminous mysteries" because Christ is the light of the world (Jn. 9: 5, n. 19). With the addition of these mysteries, all phases of our Lord's life are covered in the Rosary.

The *joyful mysteries,* which reflect on the hidden life of Christ, are "marked by *the joy radiating from the event of the Incarnation*" (n. 20). For example, in the first mystery, the Annunciation, the angel Gabriel's greeting to the Virgin Mary is linked to an invitation of messianic joy. When we meditate on the joyful mysteries, we consider the ultimate causes and the deepest meaning of Christian joy. "Mary leads us to discover the secret of Christian joy, reminding us that Christianity is, first and foremost *euangelion,* 'good news,' which has as its heart and its whole content the person of Jesus Christ, the Word made flesh, the one Savior of the world" (n. 20).

The *luminous mysteries* cover the years of our Lord's public life when he proclaims the Gospel of the

Kingdom. The Pope singles out five mysteries during this phase of Christ's life: "(1) his Baptism in the Jordan, (2) his self-manifestation at the wedding feast of Cana, (3) his proclamation of the Kingdom of God, with his call to conversion, (4) his Transfiguration, and finally, (5) his institution of the Eucharist as the sacramental expression of the Pascal Mystery" (n. 21). These mysteries reveal the Kingdom of God present in the very person of Jesus. We see that he is the Son of God, that he performs miracles, and that he inaugurates a ministry of mercy through his invitation to repentance. Christ's institution of the Eucharist testifies to his love for humanity for whose salvation he will offer himself in sacrifice (n. 21).

The *sorrowful mysteries* focus on the events of the Passion where we find "*the culmination of the revelation of God's love* and the source of our salvation" (n. 22). "The sorrowful mysteries help the believer to relive the death of Jesus, to stand at the foot of the Cross beside Mary, to enter with her into the depths of God's love for man and to experience all its life giving power" (n. 22).

The *glorious mysteries*, which contemplate the Risen One, enable Christians to rediscover the reasons for their faith and to relive the joy of the disciples upon seeing the glorified Christ. "The glorious mysteries thus lead the faithful to greater hope for the eschatological goal towards which they journey as members of the pilgrim People of God in history. This can only impel them to bear courageous witness to that 'good news' which gives meaning to their entire existence" (n. 23).

Meditating on the mysteries of the Rosary awakens in the soul a thirst for a greater knowledge of Christ and thus leads one to the Gospel. It also enables us to perceive in Christ the truth about man because Christ reveals man to himself. For example, in contemplating Christ's birth, we learn of the sanctity of life; seeing the household of Nazareth, we learn the original truth of the family according to God's plan; following him on his way to Calvary, we learn the meaning of salvific suffering; and contemplating Christ and Mary in glory, we see the ultimate goal towards which we are called (n. 25).

Saying the Rosary with Devotion.

The methodology of the Rosary is based on the repetition characteristic of acts of human love. "To understand the Rosary, one has to enter into the psychological dynamic proper to love" (n. 26). Thus the Rosary marks the "'rhythm of human life,' bringing it into harmony with the 'rhythm' of God's own life" (n. 25).

In order to deepen one's meditation, the Holy Father recommends that, after announcing each mystery, one recite a related Biblical passage (n. 30). For example, for the Annunciation, one could recall the words, "Behold the handmaid of the Lord, be it done unto me according to thy word" (Lk. 1: 38). One should then pause for a moment of silence to focus one's attention on the mystery before beginning the vocal prayers (n. 31).

Each decade of the Rosary begins with an *Our Father* to lift the mind towards God the Father. Jesus leads us to the Father and makes us brothers and sisters of himself and of one another (n. 32). The *Hail Marys* are the main element of the Rosary. The *Hail Mary* is Christological because it draws our attention to the Word made flesh. The *Glory Be* that ends each decade signifies that Christ is the way that leads to the Father in the Spirit. We thus "encounter the mystery of the three divine Persons, to whom all praise, worship and thanksgiving are due" (n. 34). After the completion of the five or more decades, the Rosary may be ended with the *Hail Holy Queen* or the *Litany of Loreto* (n. 37).

The traditional aid used for the recitation of the Rosary is a set of beads. They evoke the unending path of contemplation as well as the bond of communion that unites us all in Christ (n. 36).

If the entire Rosary cannot be said, the Holy Father recommends that the joyful mysteries be said on Mondays and Saturdays, the luminous mysteries on Thursdays, the sorrowful mysteries on Tuesdays and Fridays, and the glorious mysteries on Wednesdays and Sundays (n. 38).

If prayed properly, "the Rosary truly becomes a spiritual itinerary in which Mary acts as Mother, Teacher and Guide, sustaining the faithful by her powerful intercession" (n. 37).

Praying for Peace and for the Family.

In addition to being a prayer of meditation, the Rosary is a prayer of supplication (n. 16). The Pope especially entrusts the power of this prayer to the cause of peace in the world and the cause of the family.

"*The Rosary is by its nature a prayer for peace,* since it consists in the contemplation of Christ, the Prince of Peace, the one who is 'our peace' (Eph. 2: 14) " (n. 40). The Rosary has a peaceful effect on those who pray it, and it disposes them to spread that true peace which is a special gift of the Risen Lord. The Rosary gives us confidence that the difficult battle for peace in the world can be won.

The Rosary has always been "*a prayer of and for the family*" (n. 41). We need to increase the amount of family prayer because the *"family that prays together stays together"* (n. 41). When the members of a family come together in prayer, they "regain the ability to look one another in the eye, to communicate, to show solidarity, to forgive one another and to see their covenant of love renewed in the Spirit of God" (n. 41). The Rosary is particularly helpful for the spiritual growth and development of children. Parents should pray the Rosary *for* their children and *with* their children from their earliest years so that they can experience this daily "pause for prayer" (n. 42).

Because it is a treasure to be rediscovered by families and all of the faithful, John Paul urges everyone to "confidently take up the Rosary once again" (n. 43).

The Holy Father concludes the apostolic letter with a prayer by Blessed Bartolo Longo: "O Blessed Rosary of Mary, sweet chain which unites us to God, bond of love which unites us to the angels, tower of salvation against the assaults of Hell, safe port in our universal shipwreck, we will never abandon you" (n. 43).

Mane Nobiscum Domine
(Stay With Us Lord).
Apostolic Letter dated October 7, 2004.

This apostolic letter was issued by Pope John Paul II at the beginning of the Year of the Eucharist, October 2004 - October 2005. Its title comes from the words of the two disciples going to Emmaus who said to the Risen Christ after he had explained the Scriptures, "Stay with us, Lord, for it is almost evening" (cf., Lk. 24: 29). Christ agreed, and later the disciples recognized him in the "breaking of the bread," that is, the Eucharist. In the mystery of the Holy Eucharist, Christ is with us on our earthly journey. "[T]he divine Wayfarer continues to walk at our side, opening to us the Scriptures and leading us to a deeper understanding of the mysteries of God" (n. 2).

The Holy Eucharist has always been at the center of the Church's life. The Holy Father dedicated an entire year to the Eucharist in order "to call the whole Church to contemplate, praise, and adore in a special way this ineffable Sacrament" (n. 29). The purpose of this apostolic letter is to explain the significance of the Year of the Eucharist and to help the faithful "experience it in a deeper and more fruitful way" (n. 10).

The Eucharist: A Mystery of Light.

The Eucharist is a mystery of light because hidden in it is Christ, the "light of the world" (Jn. 8: 12, n. 11). At the "table of the Word" in the Mass the faithful are enlightened by Christ speaking to them through the Scripture readings (n. 13). The word of God permits the believers to recognize Christ just as the two disciples were able to recognize Christ after he explained the luminous message of the Scriptures to them (n. 14).

At the "table of the Bread" in the Mass we see the dimension of the Eucharist as a meal. "As such, it expresses the fellowship which God wishes to establish with us and which we ourselves must build with one another" (n. 15).

The Eucharist also has a sacrificial meaning. "In the Eucharist Christ makes present to us anew *the sacrifice offered once for all on Golgotha*" (n. 15).

In addition the Eucharist looks to the future when Christ will come in glory. This "eschatological" aspect of the Eucharist "fills our Christian journey with hope" (n. 15).

All of the dimensions of the Eucharist come together in "*the mystery of the 'real' presence*" (n. 16). We believe that Jesus "becomes substantially present, whole and entire, in the reality of his body and blood. Faith demands that we approach the Eucharist fully aware that we are approaching Christ himself" (n. 16).

The Eucharistic liturgy must always be celebrated in a dignified manner and in accordance with established norms. Singing and liturgical music should always be suitably "sacred" (n. 17).

Our awareness of Christ's real presence should be reflected by our respectful behavior at Mass and in the worship of the Eucharist outside of the Mass (n. 18). When we pray before the Blessed Sacrament, we should make reparation for the acts of carelessness and neglect—and even insults—which our Savior must endure in many places (n. 18).

The Eucharist: Source of Communion and Mission.

"Receiving the Eucharist means entering into a profound communion with Jesus" (n. 19). It "*enables us*

to have a certain foretaste of heaven on earth" (n. 19).
When we are united to Christ in communion, we are
united to the Body of Christ, the Church. As St. Paul
states, "Because there is one bread, we who are many
are one body, for we all partake of the one bread" (1
Cor. 10: 17, n. 20).

"The Eucharist is both the *source* of ecclesial unity
and its greatest *manifestation*" (n. 21). The unity of
the faithful in "one heart and one soul" (Acts 4: 32)
is manifested in a special way at Sunday Mass. Priests
should be especially attentive to Sunday Mass as the
celebration that visibly brings together the entire
parish community (n. 23).

Just as the two disciples of Emmaus set out immediately after recognizing the Lord (cf., Lk 24: 33), we
should share with others the joy we have experienced in the Eucharist. Partaking of our Lord's body
and blood is an "*urgent summons to testimony and evangelization*" (n. 24). Upon leaving Mass we must take
up our divine mandate to spread the Gospel and
imbue society with Christian values (n. 24). "In the
Year of the Eucharist Christians ought to be committed
to bearing more forceful witness to God's presence
in the world. We should not be afraid to speak about
God and to bear proud witness to our faith" (n. 26).

"Eucharist" means "thanksgiving." The Eucharist
reminds us that "*human reality cannot be justified without reference to the Creator*" (n. 26). In the midst of a
secularized culture characterized by forgetfulness of
God and a vain pursuit of human self-sufficiency, we
must give thanks to God for all that we have and all
that we are (n. 26).

In addition to be being an expression of communion within the Church, the Eucharist is a sign
and instrument of the unity of the whole human race
(n. 27). The Eucharist is "*a great school of peace*" (n. 27).

The Christian who has taken part in the Eucharist should be a *"promoter of communion, peace and solidarity* in every situation" (n. 27). He should be committed "to building a more just and fraternal society" (n. 28). Following Christ's example of washing the feet of the apostles (Jn. 13: 1-20), he should respond with fraternal charity to the many forms of poverty present in the world. "[B]y our mutual love and, in particular, by our concern for those in need we will be recognized as true followers of Christ" (n. 28).

The Holy Father concludes the apostolic letter by saying, "May the *Year of the Eucharist* be for everyone a precious opportunity to grow in awareness of the incomparable treasure which Christ has entrusted to his Church. May it encourage a more lively and fervent celebration of the Eucharist, leading to a Christian life transformed by love" (n. 29).

He calls on Mary, "woman of the Eucharist," to help "the Church discover anew enthusiasm for her mission and come to acknowledge ever more fully that the Eucharist is the source and summit of her entire life" (n. 31).

The Rapid Development.
Apostolic Letter dated January 24, 2005.

This apostolic letter, the last major pronouncement of Pope John Paul II, commemorates the fortieth anniversary of the publication of *Inter Mirifica*, the Decree on the Media of Social Communications of Vatican II, promulgated on December 4, 1963. The Holy Father reflects on the challenges that the rapidly developing technologies of the communications media pose for the Church and society. He urges the faithful to take full advantage of the Internet and other powerful means of communication to spread the Gospel. He also challenges them to integrate the message of salvation into the new culture created by such technologies.

As the "Areopagus of modern times," the media are playing a major role in unifying humanity and transforming it into a "global village" (n. 3). For many, the media have become the principal means of guidance and inspiration for one's personal, family and social behavior. The significant amounts of time people spend with the media have a major impact on the formation of personality and conscience, the structuring of affective relationships, and the development of social, political and economic life. Thus culture itself is being molded by the media (n. 3).

If they are to be used ethically and responsibly, the media must be "founded upon the supreme criteria of truth and justice" (n. 3). "The mass media can and must promote justice and solidarity according to an organic and correct vision of human development by reporting events accurately and truthfully, analyzing situations and problems completely, and providing a forum for different opinions" (n. 3).

Christ the "Communicator."

The media can look to the Incarnate Word for an example of how to communicate properly. In the Gospel we see how Jesus "explains the Scriptures, expresses himself in parables, dialogues within the intimacy of the home, speaks in the squares, along the streets, on the shores of the lake and on the mountain tops" (n. 5).

Jesus teaches that communication is a moral act. "I tell you, on the Day of Judgment people will render an account for every careless word they speak. By your words you will be acquitted, and by your words you will be condemned" (Mt. 12: 36-37, n. 13). Because of sin, man's ability to communicate with God and others was injured. Christ's Redemption, however, healed the communicative capacity of believers. Christ made it possible for man to enter into the life of the Holy Trinity which consists of the continuous "communication of perfect and infinite love among the Father, the Son and the Holy Spirit" (n. 6). In the Word made flesh, communication takes on its most profound meaning: man is able to receive the message of salvation and proclaim it to others (n. 4).

The Church is called to communicate to all of humanity the joyful message of salvation. "Go into the whole world and proclaim the gospel to every creature" (Mk. 16: 15). "For this reason the Church takes advantage of the opportunities offered by the communications media as pathways providentially given by God to intensify communication and to render more penetrating the proclamation of His word" (n. 6).

The media aid the Church in spreading the Gospel and religious values, promoting ecumenical dialogue and cooperation, and defending the moral and ethical principles that are indispensable for

Apostolic Letters   193 building a society that respects human dignity and promotes the common good (n. 7).

Redeeming the Media.

Unfortunately, the media can be, and often are, used negatively. They can silence the Gospel message in men's hearts (n. 7). For this reason, the media themselves are in need of Christ's Redemption. The inappropriate use of the media should be offset by high quality programs that respect the moral law and are rich in human and Christian values (n. 8).

An effort must be made to insure "that media professionals receive the necessary formation and pastoral attention to confront the particular tensions and ethical dilemmas that arise in their daily work" (n. 9). At the same time users of the media, especially young people, must be taught how to use the media intelligently and appropriately (n. 11).

Because of their impact on society, the media must be governed by a framework of rights and duties established by public laws and institutional codes. Everyone, however, is responsible for insuring that the media develop positively and serve the common good (n. 10). "The greatest challenge of our time for believers and for all people of good will is that of maintaining truthful and free communication which will help consolidate the integral progress of the world" (n. 13). Social issues must be resolved through constructive and open dialogue among correctly informed and discerning members of the community (n. 12).

In confronting the challenges posed by the new media culture, the Holy Father says, "Do not be afraid of the new technologies! ... Do not be afraid of being opposed by the world! ... Do not be afraid of your own weaknesses and inadequacy! The Divine Master has said, '*I am with you always, until the end of the world*' (Mt. 28: 20)" (n. 14).

John Paul concludes the apostolic letter by exhorting the faithful to "communicate the message of Christ's hope, grace and love, keeping always alive in this passing world, the eternal perspective of heaven, a perspective which no communications medium can ever directly communicate" (n. 14). He urges the faithful to pray to the Blessed Virgin Mary to "help us to communicate by every means the beauty and joy of life in Christ our Savior" (n. 14).

Letter to Families.
Letter dated February 2, 1994.

In this letter, which was written in conjunction with the United Nations International Year of the Family (1994), Pope John Paul II reflects on what it means to be a Christian family. He maintains that the "family is placed at the center of the great struggle between good and evil, between life and death, between love and all that is opposed to love" (n. 24). In many places today, the family is exposed to adverse cultural, social and economic influences "which threaten its inner unity and strength, and even stand in the way of its very formation" (n. 3).

Beginning the letter with the salutation "Dear Families!" the Holy Father figuratively knocks on the doors of families in every part of the world to personally express the Church's constant love and concern for them. The Church considers serving the family and promoting its dignity to be among her essential duties (n. 2). The truth about marriage and the family is one of her "great treasures" (n. 23). With the grace of the Holy Spirit and by following the Church's teachings, each family can be united in truth and love.

The Marital Covenant.

"Marriage, the sacrament of matrimony, is a covenant of persons in love" (n. 7). God said to Adam and Eve, "Increase and multiply and fill the earth and subdue it" (Gen. 1: 28, n. 6). Just as God created man as male and female in his own image and likeness, human fatherhood and motherhood contain an essential likeness to God. The family itself is "like God" in that it is a "community of persons united in love" (n. 6). Thus the primordial model of the family is God himself in the Trinitarian mystery (n. 6).

In the marriage ceremony each spouse says to the other, "I will love you and honor you all the days of my life" (n. 10). Such words of marital consent define the common good of the spouses which is "love, fidelity, honor, and the permanence of their union until death" (n. 10). "The good of both, which is at the same time the good of each, must then become the good of the children" (n. 10).

In becoming parents, the husband and wife are partners with God who creates each new human soul. "Cooperating with God to call new human beings into existence means contributing to the transmission of that divine image and likeness" (n. 8). "Like his parents, the new human being is also called to live as a person; he is called to a life 'in truth and love'" (n. 9).

Man is the only creature on earth whom God willed "for its own sake," that is, as an end unto himself (n. 9). The family, more than any other human reality, is the place where an individual can exist "for himself." This is why the family will always be the irreplaceable "sanctuary of life" (n. 11).

A newborn child is the embodiment of the love of the spouses. He or she is a priceless gift to the parents, as well as to the brothers and sisters, and contributes to both the common good and the community of the family (n. 11).

Maintaining a spirit of communion in a family is both a task and a challenge. The Pope emphasizes that marriage requires constant self-giving. This reflects the fundamental nature of man who is called to serve the truth in love. Man finds lasting happiness and fulfillment only in the sincere gift of self (n. 11). Selfishness will be minimized if married couples turn to God for the power to be continually renewed in love (n. 7).

The indissolubility of marriage flows from the fact that it consists of a reciprocal giving of self. "By its very nature the gift of the person must be lasting and irrevocable" (n. 11). A husband or wife cannot take back what no longer belongs to him or her.

A man and woman united in marriage are called to live as images of God in both body and spirit. "When they are united by the conjugal covenant in such a way as to become 'one flesh' (Gen. 2: 24), their union ought to take place 'in truth and love,' and thus express the maturity proper to persons created in the image and likeness of God" (n. 8). The Holy Father reaffirms that the "two dimensions of the conjugal union, the unitive and the procreative, cannot be artificially separated without damaging the deepest truth of the conjugal act itself" (n. 12).

John Paul exhorts Catholics to reaffirm this teaching in spite of pressure from contemporary society to the contrary. He urges the faithful to be willing to courageously "swim against the tide" (n. 12). "[T]he Church is convinced that she must remain absolutely faithful to the truth about human love. Otherwise she would betray herself" (n. 11).

The Civilization of Love.

The family is fundamental to achieving what Pope Paul VI called a "civilization of love" (n. 13). In fact the family is its heart and center. The alternative to a culture of love is a destructive anti-civilization dominated by utilitarianism – a civilization of *things* and not of *persons*. Women can be viewed as objects, and children can be viewed as a hindrance to the parents' supposed freedom rather than as gifts from

God (n. 13). This mentality will result in a loss of truth, a loss of love, and a loss of freedom.

The Holy Father refers to certain sex education programs as symptomatic of this utilitarian mentality. "A civilization inspired by a conformist, anti-birth mentality is not and can never be a civilization of love" (n. 13).

The hymn to love contained in the First Letter to the Corinthians remains the Magna Carta of the civilization of love. By saying that love is patient and kind and endures all things, St. Paul indicates that love is demanding (1 Cor. 13: 4, 7, n. 14). The main danger faced by love is selfishness. One manifestation of selfishness is an excessive individualism – an egocentric attitude whereby one tries to make his own rules rather than accept the law of God (n. 14).

The Fourth Commandment, "Honor your father and your mother," deals with the solidarity of the family as a community of persons. To "honor" means to acknowledge the *person* of the father, mother, and each member of the family. "Honor is essentially an attitude of unselfishness" (n. 15). In the sense that it implies a "sincere gift of person to person," honor converges with love (n. 15). The individual members of the family must be loved for their own sake since they are willed by God for their own sake (n. 9). Family stability requires a commitment of mutual respect between husband and wife and between parents and children. Such respect facilitates togetherness which is the good *par excellence* of marriage and of the family (n. 15).

A spirit of prayer will increase the family's strength and spiritual unity (n. 4). "[P]rayer needs to become a regular habit in the daily life of each family" (n. 10).

Raising children is a genuine apostolate (n. 16). Giving children a proper religious education will permit the family to become a source of evangelization in the community. Parents are the first and most important educators of their children. They cannot, however, raise them alone. There should be solidarity among families so that they may help one another. This mutual assistance is facilitated by associations of families for families (n. 16).

Society has an obligation to protect the institution of marriage and strengthen it. The state must recognize the value of a woman's work in the home because the toil associated with such work is comparable to that of any professional work (n. 17).

Christ the Bridegroom.

Our Lord must be a member of every Christian home. His presence at the wedding feast at Cana was an expression of his love for families (n. 5). His re-establishment of the indissolubility of marriage, as it was in "the beginning" (Mt. 19: 8), provided the foundation for the common good of the family (n. 18).

St. Paul describes marriage as a "great mystery" (Eph. 5: 32). He indicates the high degree of love demanded in marriage when he says, "Husbands love your wives, as Christ loved the Church and gave himself up for her ... " (Eph. 5: 25-26, n. 19). Because Christ the Bridegroom loved "to the end" (cf., Jn. 13: 1), husbands and wives can love to the end if they share in Christ's love (n. 19).

The Holy Father concludes the letter by urging families to look to the Holy Family of Nazareth as a model and by calling on Mary, Mother of Fairest Love, and St. Joseph, Guardian of the Redeemer, to accompany them with their constant protection (n. 23).

Letter to Artists.
Letter dated April 4, 1999.

In this letter addressed to artists, including poets, writers, painters, sculptors, architects, musicians and actors, Pope John Paul II addresses such questions as: How do artists contribute to the good of society? What is the relationship between art and faith? Does the Church need artists? Do artists need the Church?

The Artist, Image of God the Creator.

The Pope begins the letter, which was issued on Easter Sunday 1999, with a quotation from Genesis: "God saw all that he had made, and it was very good" (Gen. 1: 31). Because the world is good, it is also beautiful. Beauty is the visible aspect of goodness and truth. When artists create something beautiful, they capture some glimmer of the divine splendor present in creation. They go below the material surface to the spiritual core of being. Whereas the Creator brings something out of nothing (*ex nihilo*), the craftsman uses something that already exists and gives it a new form and meaning (n. 1).

God made man in his image and gave him the task of dominating the earth (Gen. 1: 28). In doing so, God committed man to the craftsman's task. Man accomplishes this task by shaping the wondrous material of his own humanity and by exercising creative dominion over the universe that surrounds him. In carrying out this work, human creatures share in God's creative power. "Not all are called to be artists in the specific sense of the term. [But] all men and women are entrusted with the task of crafting their own life: in a certain sense, they are to make of it a work of art, a masterpiece" (n. 2). Our life will be a beautiful work of art if we strive to live the Christian virtues and seek personal holiness.

The Artist and the Common Good.

What is the function of art in society? The Holy Father maintains that society needs artists because "they not only enrich the cultural heritage of each nation and of all humanity, but they also render an exceptional social service in favor of the common good" (n. 4). Vatican II states that literature and the arts have great importance in human life because they "seek to probe the true nature of man, his problems and experiences, as he strives to know and perfect himself and the world, to discover his place in history and the universe, to portray his miseries and joys, his needs and strengths, with a view to a better future" (n. 11).

Beauty, like truth, brings joy to the human heart in a world so full of tears. The Polish poet, Cyprian Norwid, wrote that "beauty is to enthuse us for work, and work is to raise us up" (n. 3). The beauty that results from the artist's creative inspiration stirs the viewer to wonder at the marvel of the universe. From this wonder comes enthusiasm for life. Enthusiasm is a critical help in overcoming life's difficulties. "Thanks to this enthusiasm, humanity, every time it loses its way, will be able to lift itself up and set out again on the right path" (n. 16). Perhaps this is what Dostoyevsky meant when he said, "Beauty will save the world" (n. 16).

Thus art has an important role in daily life for ourselves, our families and our communities. It not only gives joy to life, it inspires us to persevere in seeking the true and the good—and ultimately, God.

The Relationship between the Art and the Gospel.

As indicated above, every true work of art in some way makes visible the invisible world of the spirit. "Every genuine artistic intuition goes beyond what the senses perceive and, reaching beneath reality's surface, strives to interpret its hidden mystery. The intuition itself springs from the depths of the human soul, where the desire to give meaning to one's own life is joined by the fleeting vision of beauty and the mysterious unity of things" (n. 6).

Art and faith are partners that enrich each other. Art helps faith by helping man to find God. Things of beauty are the footprints of God which, if followed, lead to him. "Every genuine art form in its own way is a path to the inmost reality of man and the world. It is therefore a wholly valid approach to the realm of faith, which gives human experience its ultimate meaning" (n. 6).

The Church needs art to help communicate the message entrusted to her by Jesus Christ. After the Edict of Constantine legalized Christianity in the Roman Empire in 313, art became a means of expressing the Faith. Western culture reflects this expression in painting, sculpture, architecture, music, poetry, and literature. For example, in the great basilicas and other buildings for worship, "the functional is wedded to the creative impulse inspired by a sense of the beautiful and the intuition of mystery" (n. 8). The forms of Christian architecture, including Romanesque, Byzantine, Gothic, and Baroque, portray "not only the genius of the artist, but [also] the soul of a people" (n. 8).

Thus, Christian art evokes in a sensory way the mystery of the Incarnation, the Word made flesh. Artistic representations of Gospel scenes have always been a means of catechesis. At the same time, the Gospel helps art by being a source of inspiration for it (n. 7).

Even where artists are non-believers, "art remains a kind of bridge to religious experience. In so far as it seeks the beautiful ... art is by its nature a kind of appeal to the mystery. Even when they explore the darkest depths of the soul or the most unsettling aspects of evil, artists give voice in a way to the universal desire for redemption" (n. 10).

The Pope ends the letter by invoking the intercession of Mary, who is *tota pulchra* (all beautiful) and who has been portrayed by countless artists. He prays that artists will use their talents "to affirm that true beauty which, as a glimmer of the Spirit of God, will transfigure matter, opening the human soul to the sense of the eternal" (n. 16).

Letter to the Elderly.

Letter dated October 1, 1999.

The United Nations designated 1999 as the International Year of Older Persons. This letter, issued by Pope John Paul II for such occasion, provides a vision of spiritual maturity for the elderly. Writing as an older person himself, the Holy Father urges the elderly to see the providential and merciful hand of God during this season of their lives. He maintains that the struggles and tribulations they experience can, with God's grace, contribute to their continued growth in character and holiness (n. 1). Life should be valued as God's primordial gift in every age, including old age (n. 16).

Members of the Pope's generation lived through much of the twentieth century which was marked by both lights and shadows. It witnessed unprecedented sufferings that affected the lives of many millions of people. Such sufferings resulted from the two world wars, the cold war, many regional conflicts, extreme poverty in many parts of the world, and the systematic violation of human rights by dictatorial regimes (n. 3).

The century also saw positive developments for mankind such as a growing consciousness of universal human rights, a greater perception of the value of democracy, an increasing recognition of the dignity of women, and tremendous progress in medicine and science. These developments are sources of hope as the Third Millennium begins (n. 4).

The Inexorable Passage of Time.

As the Roman poet Virgil put it, "time flies irretrievably" (n. 2). John Paul exhorts his contemporaries "to meditate on how quickly time flies, not in order to resign ourselves to an inexorable fate, but rather to make full use of the years we still have before us" (n. 4).

We see in the Old Testament that God gave special missions to a number of elderly people such as Abraham, Sarah, Moses, and Eleazer. Similarly, many New Testament figures were "advanced in years" (Lk. 1: 7) including Elizabeth, Zechariah, Simeon, and Nicodemus. "They remind us that at every stage in life the Lord can ask each of us to contribute what talents we have. The service of the Gospel has nothing to do with age!" (n. 7).

The Bible presents old age as a favorable time for bringing life to its fulfillment. It is a time when everything comes together and when the meaning of life can be grasped more fully (n. 8). Reaching old age is itself a sign of divine favor (n. 6).

Cicero referred to old age as the "autumn of life" (n. 5). "[E]ach stage in life has its own beauty and its own tasks" (n. 6). With the quieting of the passions and the accumulation of experience, old age is especially a time of greater wisdom and maturity of judgment (n. 5). The elderly can thus offer younger people valuable guidance.

Retirees have more time to devote to carrying out the Church's mission of evangelization. For example, they can teach catechism to children and visit the sick and the isolated. The elderly are able to instill courage in others by their silent prayers and their witness of suffering borne with patient acceptance (n. 13).

While the elderly can make special contributions to society, they also have a greater need of help from society. "The signs of human frailty connected with advanced age become a summons to the mutual dependence and indispensable solidarity which link the different generations, inasmuch as every person needs others and draws enrichment from the gifts and charisms of all" (n. 10).

"Honor Your Father and Your Mother."

In the past, great respect was shown to the elderly. In today's society, which gives priority to immediate usefulness and productivity, old age is often undervalued. Older people may be led to wonder whether their lives are still worthwhile (n. 9). To prevent this, the elderly should always be treated with dignity by the younger generations. For people influenced by the Bible, this is commanded by the Decalogue: "Honor your father and your mother" (n. 11). The Fourth Commandment refers not only to one's parents but to all older persons. "Where this commandment is accepted and faithfully observed, there is little danger that older people will be regarded as a useless or troublesome burden" (n. 11).

"Honoring older people involves a threefold duty: welcoming them, helping them, and making good use of their qualities" (n. 12). "There must be a growing conviction that a fully human civilization shows respect and love for the elderly, so that despite their diminishing strength, they feel a vital part of society" (n. 12). As Cicero noted, "[T]he burden of age is lighter for those who feel respected and loved by the young" (n. 12).

As the number of older people increases, it becomes more important to promote an attitude of acceptance and appreciation of the elderly and not relegate them to the fringes. The elderly should be assisted in maintaining their physical wellbeing, their intellectual development, and their personal relationships. The Holy Father commends social programs that enable older people to make themselves useful and to put their time, talents and experience at the service of others (n. 16).

"The ideal is still for the elderly to remain within the family, with the guarantee of effective social assistance for the greater needs which age or illness entail" (n. 13). At some point, however, it may become necessary for them to be admitted to "homes for the elderly" where they can enjoy the company of others and receive specialized care (n. 13).

Euthanasia has appeared as a misguided solution to difficult problems. Understood as directly causing death, euthanasia "is an intrinsically evil act, a violation of God's law and an offense against the dignity of the human person" (n. 9). It is not necessary, however, to use aggressive medical treatment to extend life in the case of a terminal illness (n. 9).

When God permits illness or loneliness to accompany old age, he also gives grace and strength to enable the elderly person to be united to the cross of Christ and thus to share more fully in God's plan of salvation. All human suffering finds meaning in the cross. We must always be convinced that God is our Father, "a Father rich in love and mercy" (n. 13).

Confronting Death.

"If life is a pilgrimage towards our heavenly home, then old age is the most natural time to look towards the threshold of eternity" (n. 14). Facing the prospect of making this passage is always difficult, however, because man was made for life, not death. Death was not part of God's original plan for mankind but came about as a consequence of sin (cf., Gen. 2: 3). "It is understandable why, when faced with this dark reality, man instinctively rebels" (n. 14).

The anticipation of death forces men and women to ask themselves fundamental questions such as, "Does death represent the definitive end of life or does something lie beyond it?" (n. 14). Jesus provides an answer by saying, "I am the resurrection and the life; he who believes in me, even if he die, shall live; and whoever lives and believes in me, shall never die" (Jn. 11: 25-26, n. 15). Christ, having crossed the threshold of death, revealed the life that lies beyond it. He is the first witness of eternal life, and in him human hope for immortality is fulfilled (n. 15).

Faith thus illuminates the mystery of death and brings serenity to old age. An eternal perspective inspires an elderly person to deepen his spiritual life through more fervent prayer and to be more committed to the service of one's brothers and sisters in charity (n. 16). The human spirit in some way remains ever young if it is oriented towards eternity (n. 12). Maintaining a youthful spirit is also facilitated by a good conscience and a concern for others. The Holy Father encourages older persons to give of themselves until the very end for sake of the Kingdom of God (n. 17).

The Pope ends the letter by saying that he finds great peace in thinking about when the Lord will call him from this life to the next. Full of hope, he calls on Mary to "pray for us now and at the hour of our death."

Incarnationis Mysterium
(The Mystery of the Incarnation).
Bull of Indiction for the Great Jubilee of the Year 2000 dated November 29, 1998.

Incarnationis Mysterium is the Bull of Indiction by which Pope John Paul II officially proclaimed that the Third Christian Millennium would begin with a Jubilee Year. A papal bull (from the Latin word *bulla* meaning "seal") is a decree with the force of ecclesiastical law. The Holy Father decreed that the Great Jubilee would begin on December 24, 1999 and end on January 6, 2001 (n. 6).

A jubilee is a special opportunity to reflect on the mystery of the Incarnation and the Redemption. It is a time to focus on the essence of Christianity and one's response to Christ's earthly life and death. The first Christian jubilee was held in 1300 (n. 5). Thousands of people from all over Europe felt the need to make a penitential pilgrimage to Rome at Christmas in 1299. Moved with admiration on seeing the pilgrims, Pope Boniface VIII declared that 1300 would be a Holy Year with special indulgences. Every Holy Year since then has been a time of internal and external renewal in the Church. The celebration for the year 2000 was a "Great" Jubilee because it marked the beginning of a new millennium.

The Pope urges the faithful, as they enter the Third Millennium, to undertake the missionary task of the Church with renewed vigor, knowing that "they bring to the world the true light, Christ the Lord. Proclaiming Jesus of Nazareth, the true God and perfect Man, the Church opens to all people the prospect of being 'divinized' and thus becoming more human" (n. 2).

John Paul compares the Jubilee celebration to an extended wedding feast (n. 4). He expresses his ardent desire that the Jubilee "may be experienced as a journey of reconciliation and a sign of true hope for all who look to Christ and to his Church, the sacrament of 'intimate union with God and the unity of the entire human race'" (n. 4). He reminds the faithful that, after the Redemption accomplished by Christ, "no one can be separated from the love of God except through his own fault" (n. 6).

The Pope indicates that the main themes of the Holy Year are: the notion of pilgrimage, the Holy Door, indulgences, the purification of memory, charity, and remembering the martyrs. All of these are "signs of the mercy of God at work in the Jubilee" (n. 11).

Pilgrimages.

We make pilgrimages in order to remember that on earth we are wayfarers on a journey to heaven. We are on a personal journey of faith that will last our entire life. Pilgrimages to Christian shrines and churches help us to renew our faith and deepen our hope for heaven. Pilgrimages should be made with a spirit of prayer and penance. They should be occasions for us to remember that God himself set out on man's earthly paths and that God should always be our traveling companion on our journey through life (n. 7).

The Holy Door.

Passing through the Holy Door of a designated Jubilee church "evokes the passage from sin to grace which every Christian is called to accomplish" (n. 8). Jesus said, "I am the door" (Jn. 10: 17). No one can come to the Father except through him. Psalm 118 can be applied only to Jesus: "This is the door of the Lord which the just may enter" (Ps. 118: 20). To pass through the Holy Door means to confess that Jesus Christ is the Lord. Just as the Holy Door leads into a church building, our faith keeps us in the Catholic Church where we receive the gifts of truth, grace and fellowship.

Indulgences.

Indulgences are expressions of God's mercy. When a repentant believer confesses his sins in the sacrament of Penance, he receives pardon and is restored to communion with God and with his Church (n. 9). He must still, however, be purified of the consequences of sin. The wounds caused by sin must be healed. This is ordinarily accomplished by "temporal punishment," the undertaking of penance on earth or suffering in Purgatory. "With an indulgence, the repentant sinner receives a remission of the temporal punishment due to the sin already forgiven" (n. 9). The merits of Christ, Mary and the saints are applied to us by the Church when she grants an indulgence to us. (Analogously, a person will overcome an infection more quickly if he takes antibiotics than if he fights the illness without them.)

A *plenary* indulgence removes *all* of the temporal punishment due to sin. A *partial* indulgence removes *some* of the temporal punishment. A plenary indulgence can be gained once a day for oneself or for a soul in Purgatory.

The Purification of Memory.

We need to ask forgiveness for our sins and for the sins of other Christians that have been a "counter-testimony" to Christianity (n. 11). We must convert to God with all our heart and renounce all sin.

Charity.

We must open our eyes to the needs of those who are poor and excluded. Overcoming poverty requires effective cooperation among peoples of every language, race, nationality and religion. "Extreme poverty is a source of violence, bitterness and scandal; and to eradicate it is to do the work of justice and therefore the work of peace" (n. 12).

Remembering the Martyrs.

The martyrs proclaimed the Gospel "by giving their lives for love" (n. 13). The 2,000 years since the birth of Christ have been marked by the continual witness of martyrs. The twentieth century had a huge number of martyrs, especially resulting from Nazism and Communism. We must pay homage to the martyrs for strengthening our faith and winning graces for us from God. We must jealously guard their memory. Martyrdom is the most eloquent proof of the truth of the Gospel.

Finally, the Holy Father urges the faithful to grow during the Jubilee in devotion to Mary, the Mother of God and the Mother of the Church, invoking her as "Mother of Mercy." Her exceptional pilgrimage of faith represents a constant point of reference for us (n. 14).

The Truth and Meaning of Human Sexuality: Guidelines for Education within the Family.

Issued by the Pontifical Council for the Family on December 8, 1995.

This document was issued by the Pontifical Council for the Family to give parents a renewed sense of confidence in educating their children about sexuality in a culture so often opposed to the Church's teaching on this subject. Although not written by Pope John Paul II, it is included in this volume because it is based primarily on his teachings which are quoted extensively.

In a word, the *truth* about human sexuality is that it is the expression in man and woman of God's life-giving love. The *meaning* of human sexuality is to lead the person to fulfillment through the gift of self in love (n. 46). A sexual act is truthful if it is a free and total gift of self to one's spouse and is open to the transmission of life.

In this document the Pontifical Council discusses: God's plan for human sexuality, how chastity preserves the true meaning of sexuality, the need for parents to play an active role in the education of their children about life, and the proper criteria for sex education programs in schools.

The Design of God for Human Sexuality.

The document begins with a description of God's plan for human love. Because man is made in the image of God who is love, man is created for love (n. 8). Just as a loving communion of persons is found in the Blessed Trinity, man is called to a loving communion with God and others. "Love is, therefore, the fundamental and innate vocation of every human being" (n. 8). Human love consists in self-giving which is essential for personal self-realization and happiness (n. 3).

According to the design of God, each human being is called to love in the unity of body and spirit. "Femininity and masculinity are complementary gifts through which human sexuality is an integrating part of the concrete capacity for love that God has inscribed in man and woman" (n. 10). The human body's capacity to express love as a gift of self is what John Paul calls the "nuptial meaning of the body" (n. 10). A true expression of nuptial love, whether in apostolic celibacy or in marriage, "fulfills the very meaning of [a person's] being and existence" (n. 10). Human sexuality is thus part of what God saw as being "very good" when He created man in His image as male and female (Gen. 1: 27, n. 11). Conjugal love in fact is a "symbol and image of God's love for us" (n. 96).

The Pontifical Council says that "sexuality has love as its intrinsic end, more precisely, love as donation and acceptance, love as giving and receiving" (n. 11). In the expression of the nuptial meaning of the body, man and woman become "partakers of the divine nature" (2 Pet. 1: 4, n. 12). They are able to love as God loves.

Nuptial love (celibate or conjugal) enriches the person, makes him or her grow, and contributes to building a civilization of love. When the meaning of gift is lacking in sexuality, however, persons are treated as things or objects. They are used as a means of another's selfish gratification. This contributes to bringing about a culture of death (n. 11).

Marriage is the communion of persons where, according to God's will, human life is conceived, grows and develops (n. 14). The parents become partners with God in giving life to a new human person (n. 15). Conjugal love is true if it is total, faithful and fruitful (open to life) (n. 29). Such conjugal love images God's life-giving love.

The vocation to apostolic celibacy requires the gift of oneself to God alone with an undivided heart (n. 12). Today's lack of vocations is a consequence of the breakdown of the family. When marriage is not esteemed, celibacy cannot exist. This is because "when human sexuality is not regarded as a great value given by the Creator, the renunciation of it for the sake of the Kingdom of Heaven loses its meaning" (n. 34).

True Love and Chastity.

Chastity is the virtue that permits man's sexuality to be an expression of God's life-giving love. One cannot make a free gift of himself if he lacks self-mastery. One must possess himself before he can give himself. Self-possession is acquired by living the virtues, especially chastity. "Chastity is a spiritual power which frees love from selfishness and aggression" (n. 16). According to the *Catechism of the Catholic Church*, "Chastity means the successful integration of sexuality within the person and thus the inner unity of man in his bodily and spiritual being" (n. 4).

The Pontifical Council states, "Chastity is the joyous affirmation of someone who knows how to live self-giving ... The chaste person is not self-centered, not involved in selfish relationships with other people. Chastity makes the personality harmonious. It matures it and fills it with inner peace. This purity of mind and body helps develop true self-respect and at the same time makes one capable of respecting others" (n. 17).

"Either man governs his passions and finds peace, or he lets himself be dominated by them and becomes unhappy" (n. 18). St. Paul teaches in numerous passages in his epistles that chastity requires rejecting sinful thoughts, words and actions (n. 18).

The Lord's redemption has made chastity possible even in the unfavorable circumstances of today's society (n. 73). If it were not possible, God's "universal call to holiness" would be in vain (n. 100). Practices which help us to grow in chastity include: guarding the senses, avoiding occasions of sin, observing modesty, making good use of time, praying with humility, frequenting the sacraments of Penance and Holy Eucharist, and having devotion to our Lady (n. 71).

Educating Children for Chastity.

Vatican II reiterated the Church's constant teaching that parents have the original, primary and inalienable right to educate their children. This includes the right to educate them in conformity with their moral and religious convictions (n. 43). Parents must reclaim their proper task of being educators of their children for chastity. They must control sex education—including what is taught in school.

To fulfill their function as educators, parents must find time to be with their children and talk with them. Their children are their most important task, more important than work, entertainment and social position (n. 51).

In order for children to be properly disposed to acquire the virtue of chastity, parents must maintain a proper atmosphere of love and virtue in the family. This involves, for example, teaching the need for privacy, correcting bad habits and controlling access to TV and the mass media. Parents must help their children understand the value of sexuality in stages. They must also help them discover their own vocation to marriage or apostolic celibacy (n. 22).

The Pontifical Council provides four principles regarding the transmission of information about sexuality by parents to their children: 1) each child is unique and must receive individualized formation (n. 65), 2) the moral dimension must always be part of explanations about sexuality with insistence on its positive value and its capacity to generate true love (n. 68), 3) formation in chastity and information about sexuality must be provided in the context of education for love (n. 70), and 4) parents should provide information regarding sexuality with delicacy, clarity and at the appropriate time (n. 75).

The document describes in detail the principle stages of a child's development. A child's early years can be the most critical ones. Young children must be taught how to practice self-denial, for example, by giving up something for Lent and by limiting snacks. "An undisciplined or spoiled child is inclined toward a certain immaturity and moral weakness in future years because chastity is difficult if a person is selfish and disordered" (n. 86).

Sex Education Programs in Schools.

The Pontifical Counsil provides practical guidelines for parents regarding sex education programs in schools. It recommends that: 1) parents should be made aware of their right and duty to educate their children on this subject (n. 114), 2) parents should associate with other parents to exercise this right (n. 115), 3) parents must keep themselves informed as to the content and methodology of what is being taught to their children in school (n. 116), and 4) parents must remove their children from programs that do not correspond to their own principles (n. 117).

Some of the key working principles and norms for the conduct of sex education programs are: 1) human sexuality is a sacred mystery and must be presented according to the doctrinal and moral teaching of the church, always bearing in mind the effects of original sin (n. 122), 2) only information proper to each phase of a child's development should be presented to him or her (n. 124), 3) no material of an erotic nature should be presented to children or young people of any age, individually or as a group (n. 126), and 4) no one should ever be invited, let alone obliged to act in any way that objectively offends against modesty or could subjectively offend against his or her own delicacy or sense of privacy (n. 127).

Parents must work to insure that the sex education programs in the Catholic or other schools their children attend are consistent with these criteria.

The Pontifical Council ends the document by urging parents to have confidence in their ability to properly educate their children for chastity. They should bear in mind our Lord's promise: "Blessed are the pure of heart for they shall see God" (Mt. 5: 8, n. 150).